NATIONAL 2ND EDITION

SIMPLE CONTRACTS for PERSONAL USE

BY ATTORNEY STEPHEN ELIAS & MARCIA STEWART

Edited by Mary Randolph
& Barbara Kate Repa

Illustrated by Linda Allison

NOLO PRESS BERKELEY, CALIFORNIA

Please Read This

Nolo Press is committed to keeping its books up-to-date. Each new printing, whether or not it is called a new edition, has been revised to reflect the latest law changes. This book was printed and updated on the date indicated below. Before you rely on information in it, you might wish to call Nolo Press (415) 549-1976 to check whether there has been a later printing or edition. It's your responsibility to check all material you have read here before relying on it.

SECOND EDITION

First Printing: September 1991

Editors: Mary Randolph
Barbara Kate Repa

Production: Stephanie Harolde
Terri Hearsh
Jackie Mancuso

Book Design: Toni Ihara

Elias, Stephen
Simple contracts for personal use / by Stephen Elias and Marcia Stewart.
p. cm.
Includes index.
ISBN 0-87337-155-0 : $16.95
1. Contracts--United States--Popular works. 2. Contracts--United States--Forms. I. Stewart, Marcia. II. Title.
KF801.Z9E545 1991
346.73'02--dc20
[347.3062]

91-17629
CIP

Dedication

To Catherine Elias Jermany for her unflagging support and contribution to this book.

Acknowledgements

We couldn't have written this book without the editorial assistance and support of Mary Randolph, Barbara Kate Repa and Jake Warner. Glen Voloshin, Toni Ihara and Terri Hearsh labored long and hard to make the book both attractive and functional. Linda Allison provided the wonderful artwork. Cynthia Kelly of NannyCare, USA in Oakland, California, Michael Mansel of Insurance Associates in Walnut Creek, California and Warren Siegel of the Berkeley based Consumers Group Legal Services were each kind enough to review relevant portions of the manuscript and offer invaluable suggestions for their improvement. David Freund hunted down and destroyed the myriad of pesky mistakes that survived the earlier drafts of the book. Our heartfelt thanks to Robin Leonard and the many wonderful people at Nolo Press whose efforts support this and the other Nolo books.

Table of Contents

Introduction

This book provides ready-to-use contracts for a variety of private transactions, including lending money to a friend or relative, selling your car or other property, storing property, boarding pets, hiring someone to repair or remodel your house, arranging in-home child care and other household help and settling minor legal disputes. Unlike contracts intended for use in the normal course of a business or commercial enterprise, which tend to contain a bewildering variety of clauses, the contracts in this book cover everyday situations in everyday (but legal) language. They are designed to provide a reasonable level of specificity without sacrificing the important virtue of simplicity.

Why Write a Contract?

The premise of this book is simple: It is almost always a good idea to put contracts that affect money, property or important legal rights into writing. This is true whether the parties are relatives, close friends or strangers. Among the obvious advantages of written agreements are that they:

- force the parties to the agreement to be specific
- better protect the parties in case one of them dies when the contract is in effect
- provide a point of reference when memories grow dim and
- satisfy the IRS in certain tax contexts.

It is particularly important to write out the details of agreements in family situations. Careless informality in this area commonly results in misunderstandings that have truly unhappy long-term consequences. For example, if a parent asks a child to execute a promissory note in exchange for a $5,000 loan, the written agreement will come in very handy 10 years down the line should the child suddenly remember the transaction as a gift rather than a loan. Similarly, if the parent dies leaving his estate equally to the kids, the note will make it clear that one child should receive a slightly smaller share. And even if confusion never develops, having the transaction reduced to writing will go a long way towards reassuring others in the family that one child isn't getting preferential treatment.

What Is a Contract?

We've mentioned the advantages of making a written contract. It's time to define our terms. Rather than giving you a law text definition, let's try a more informal and probably more meaningful one: A contract is formed when either two persons each promise to do something for the other or one person makes a promise in exchange for another person's performance of an act. A written contract consists of these promises reduced to written form. Properly used, the forms and instructions contained in this book will guide you in creating simple, easy to understand and binding contracts.

When Is a Contract Enforceable?

Most people who enter into a contract want to know if it is enforceable. Or, put more directly, if the other party doesn't perform his obligations under the contract, can you realistically either make him do so or at least recover the damages you suffer as a result of his breach?

In general, once a contract has been made, the courts (including small claims court) will enforce it unless:

a. The terms are too vague to be enforced. If a dispute arises that the parties can't straighten out on their own, the agreement must be clear and detailed enough about the parties' obligations so that an arbitrator or judge can sensibly decide who is right. The value of a contract often depends heavily on the degree to which it anticipates the problems likely to arise under it. A house painting contract providing that "Acme Painting Co. shall paint your house in exchange for $5,000" provides almost no guidance to the parties or a court. As a contract, it would be next to worthless and probably could not be enforced. On the other hand, a contract containing detailed specifications down to the type of prep work, type of primer and color of paint does provide an adequate basis for enforcement of its terms.

or

b. It involves an illegal purpose. Contracts formed to accomplish something that the law prohibits may be excellent reminders to the parties of their obligations to each other; they are not, however, enforceable in a court. For instance, if two people sign a contract under which a non-transferable lottery ticket is in fact transferred in exchange for the original holder's right to share in the proceeds of a jackpot, the agreement cannot later be taken to court for enforcement since the law prohibits the transfer.

or

c. Enforcement would be grossly unfair. The simple contracts you can make using this book are not likely to be challenged on the grounds of fairness. However, you should know that if a contract is both extremely unfair and results from one party's superior bargaining position, a court may choose not to enforce it. Just keep in mind that the best contracts benefit both parties more or less equally, and you will have no problem.

With this book it's easy to write a contract that sticks...

How Our Contracts Differ From Commercial Contracts

The contracts provided in this book are designed strictly for non-commercial purposes, that is, for transactions that don't regularly occur in the context of an ongoing business. Why do our contracts differ from business contracts? Business contracts that are drafted to cover commercial transactions for the purchase of new motor vehicles, houses or insurance usually involve a type of applied paranoia, which results in dozens of detailed clauses that attempt to anticipate all sorts of eventualities, some exceedingly remote. This is because the drafters feel they must not only set out each party's obligations, but also must plug every possible loophole through which the parties might escape. Commercial contracts are also often required by law to include a number of clauses designed to protect consumers, which our contracts don't include.

Although each of our contracts uses simple terms and is basically self-explanatory, we have provided a number of notes and examples to help you better understand various clauses. We also allow you to alter any of the contracts to better suit your particular situation. These and other tips about how to use this book are contained in Chapter 1. Please read it before proceeding to the chapter containing the agreement you wish to use.

Chapter 1

How to Use This Book

In this short chapter we tell you how to use this book. We urge you to read it carefully before proceeding to the chapter which contains the forms which interest you.

A. Overview of the Book

Each chapter deals with a specific type of contract. (See list below.) After a brief discussion of the relevant law, we present and briefly discuss a number of variations on the basic agreement. For example, in Chapter 2, which covers promissory notes, we show agreements to lend/borrow money that don't provide for interest, that do provide for interest, that allow repayment in a lump sum, that are repayable in installments, and so on. Tear-out forms for each type of contract are located at the end of that chapter.

B. The Contracts in This Book

The simple contracts provided in this book include:

- **Promissory notes:** Agreements for use when money is being lent and borrowed, when payment is deferred for an item being sold and when disputes are being settled (Chapter 2)
- **Bills of sale:** Agreements that contain the terms of sale for such large-ticket items as used cars, appliances, computers or boats (Chapter 3)
- **Storage contracts:** Agreements covering storage of property, which spell out such details as who is reponsible for damage to the property, whether the storage will be paid for and what happens if the property is abandoned (Chapter 4)
- **Releases:** Agreements to settle disputes (for example, "fender benders", contractual misunderstandings, neighbor problems, etc.), where one or both parties release the other from liability, usually in

exchange for a monetary payment. These contracts are useful for settling disputes which otherwise might end up in court (Chapter 5)

- **Home repair contracts:** Agreements designed to cover situations where a homeowner engages another to perform home repair, remodeling or landscape services (Chapter 6)
- **Child care and other household help contracts:** Agreements for hiring babysitters, au pairs and other in-home child care as well as housecleaners and other domestic workers (Chapter 7).

In the Appendix we provide a list of State Consumer Protection Offices for further information.

C. Filling In the Forms

Each of the tear-out forms in this book asks you to make certain choices by checking boxes and inserting information in blank spaces. The following instructions will help you do this correctly.

1. Typing vs. Printing

Most of you will agree that a typewritten document usually carries more weight in the real world than a handwritten one. Then too, the legibility of typewritten text is generally superior to handwriting. For these reasons we suggest that you take the time to type in the information on the form that is to be signed by the parties. Drafts, of course, can be filled in by hand. If, however, convenience or cost dictates that the document be filled in by hand, take the time to neatly print it.

2. Describing Events And Property

Some of the forms ask you to describe events or property. For property, list the make, model, type, color, identifying number if it has one and any other identifying characteristics that come to mind. For instance, if a computer is involved, you might say "IBM PC XT, ID # 445556, 20 MB hard disk." If a motorcycle is the subject of the transaction, your description would be something like, "1984 red Honda 500 Superhawk I.D. # 55565433, Montana Lic. # 567891." There are no magic words here. Your only objective is to adequately identify the property so that no misunderstanding can later arise as to what was intended.

The same is true for events. As long as in specifying an event you mention the date, time (if known), location, and include a sentence about what happened, your description should be adequate. Where we think it useful, we have provided several examples of appropriate descriptions.

3. Selecting from Several Choices

Many of the forms contain one or more clauses which ask you to choose among several options. For instance, the following clause, taken from our simple home repairs contract (Chapter 6), asks you to select the method of payment for the work being performed:

---

2. Payment Terms

In exchange for the specified work, Homeowner agrees to pay Contractor as follows:

[Choose one and check the appropriate boxes]

☐ a. $ ________________, payable by ☐ cash ☐ check upon completion of the specified work.

☐ b. $ ________________, payable by ☐ cash ☐ check one half at the beginning of the specified work and one half at the completion of the specified work.

☐ c. $ ________________ per hour for each hour of work performed, up to a maximum of $ ________________ payable at the following times and in the following manner:

____

____

When you are presented with a clause like this, simply check the correct box. If the box you select asks for additional information, don't forget to provide it. When you can choose more than one box in a sequence we tell you to "choose one or more of the following." When we want you to only select one, we tell you to "choose one."

4. Changing and Deleting Clauses

Because our contracts are form contracts, some clauses may not apply to your situation. If this happens, put N.A. (for "not applicable") at the beginning of the blank line (the first line if there is more than one). If you want to remove a whole clause from a contract, clearly cross it out and have both parties put their initials next to it. If you want to change some language, cross out what you don't want, clearly insert the language you wish to substitute, and initial the changes. Because many of our forms are designed to be used both by individual and joint users, you may occasionally encounter some awkward language structure, such as "Promisor(s)," "☐ We ☐ I," and "his/hers." Leaving the language as is will not affect the validity of the notes. However, you may wish to ink out the portion of the structure that doesn't apply to your situation. If so, you need not initial the change since it is technical rather than substantive in nature. As we've seen, there is no requirement that a contract be totally neat or even that it be typewritten. On the other hand, it should be clearly legible. Therefore, if your product gets a little too messy, it is best to retype or carefully reprint the entire agreement before signing it.

5. Additions To Forms

Although the forms are presented to you as more or less complete contracts, there may be times when no one form will precisely fit your situation. Does this mean that you need to go out and look for another book? Not necessarily. First, most of our contracts (promissory notes and releases excepted) provide space for you to write in additional terms. Second, you can mix and match the provisions found in any of our forms and add your own as well. If you are willing to retype your own agreement from scratch, your options are virtually unlimited.

Now that we have suggested how free you are to arrive at your own agreement, we want to give you a heartfelt warning. If you do strike out on your own, please remember that it is easy to create self-contradictory contracts which can lead to a lot of head scratching and defeat the purpose of putting your agreement in writing in the first place. So be very careful to check that your final product is:

- easy to understand
- free from ambiguity and
- internally consistent.

6. If you Need More Space

Although we have tried to leave adequate space for you to enter information, you may run out of room on occasion. If so, take the following steps:

a. The first place you run out of room, put "Continued on attachment 1" at the end of the space on the form. The second place you run out of room put "Continued on attachment 2." Use a separate attachment each time you need more room.

b. For each attachment, title a piece of 8 1/2" by 11" white blank paper with the word "Attachment" and the proper number (that is, Attachment 1 for the first attachment, and so on). On the next line below this title, put the word "Continuation" and the number and subject matter of the clause from the main contract which you are continuing (for example, "Continuation of clause #4, defects in property").

c. Type or print the additional information on this page.

d. Sign or initial the page (both parties) at the end of the added material.

e. Attach the page to the main contract.

f. If there is more than one page, number the pages and refer to the proper page numbers in the blanks on the main form.

D. Using the Book

To get the best use out of this book, we suggest you proceed in this manner:

1. Identify the chapter you need from the table of contents.
2. Read all of the introductory material and skim the sample form agreements.
3. Select the form most appropriate for you.
4. Make at least two good photocopies (both sides if appropriate).
5. Turn back to the introductory material for that chapter and read it carefully to make sure you are using the agreement in its correct context and haven't overlooked anything.
6. Use one of the photocopies to make a rough draft.
7. When you are satisfied, prepare a final version on the other photocopy by typing or neatly printing your entries.
8. Make a photocopy of your final version.
9. Sign and date both the photocopy and original and have the other party also date and sign them (he need not sign on the same day you do).
10. Provide the other party with the original or photocopy, keeping the other one for your own records.
11. Store your copy of the contract in a safe place.[1]

NOTARIZATION NOTE: None of the contracts in this book need be signed in front of a notary. On the other hand, if you feel that having an agreement notarized will add to its importance in your situation, it can't hurt. Notaries can usually be found in banks, real estate offices, courts and law offices.

[1] *For the Record,* a computer program published by Nolo Press, can provide invaluable assistance in helping you keep track of your contracts as well as other important records. See back of book for order information.

Chapter 2

Promissory Notes—Written Evidence of a Debt

Have you ever borrowed money from a friend and signed something that said "I owe you $100"? If you have, you have executed a promissory note. A basic promissory note is nothing more than a written promise to pay money to someone. Of course, as with all legal documents, promissory notes may contain dozens of "wherefores," "but fors" and "what ifs." However, because the notes set out in this book are designed to be used primarily between family and friends, we tend toward the simple.

WARNING: The notes provided in this chapter are designed for use in personal and family contexts where the parties know each other. They should not be used in a commercial context as part of the ongoing sale of goods or services, or when money is lent to a stranger and the primary motivation is to collect interest. Why not? Because state and federal laws impose special requirements on notes executed by banks, loan companies and other commercial entities that lend money in the regular course of their business. Accordingly, such notes typically contain legal provisions that are not appropriate or required for most non-commercial situations and often must set out various warnings in large bold type. If despite our warning you feel one or more of our agreements is adequate for your business purposes, check it with a lawyer first.

A. General Function of Promissory Notes

The primary function of a promissory note is to serve as written evidence of a debt, typically when money is borrowed or something is bought on credit (for example, you take the computer home today but pay for it next month). Perhaps in the best of all possible worlds, such evidence would not be needed. One friend would loan another $1,000 and shake hands on it, and that's it. However, because the "best possible world" and the "real world" often are barely on speaking terms, we believe it is essential that promissory notes be put in writing.

For example, in the real world people die. What happens if either the lender or borrower dies before the debt is repaid? If it's the borrower who dies first, his estate will owe the sum in question; if it's the lender, her estate is entitled to its payment. Yet, if there is no written evidence of the debt, it may well never be paid or collected. Among the other contingencies that can intervene between the time money is borrowed and the time it is supposed to be repaid are:

- bankruptcy
- divorce
- physical or mental illness
- changes in IRS rules governing loans and
- a souring of the relationship between the parties.

Enough said, we hope.

B. Types of Promissory Notes in This Chapter

This chapter contains six tear-out, negotiable[1] promissory notes:

FORM 1: Note to Borrow/Lend Money Repayable in Lump Sum Without Interest.[2]

FORM 2: Note to Borrow/Lend Money Repayable in Lump Sum With Interest.

FORM 3: Note to Borrow/Lend Money Repayable in Installments Without Interest.

FORM 4: Note to Borrow/Lend Money Repayable in Installments With Interest.

FORM 5: Note to Borrow/Lend Money Repayable in Lump Sum and Secured by Interest in Real or Personal Property.

FORM 6: Note to Borrow/Lend Money Repayable in Installments and Secured by Interest in Real or Personal Property.

We also include a monthly payment record (FORM 7) to keep track of payments made under installment notes.

C. Sample Uses For Notes

Before we discuss each of these notes in more detail, let's take a moment to examine how they might be used. Perhaps the best way to do this is by use of an extended example. So please meet Morris Jones and his family.

Morris lives in Austin, Texas with his wife Julie, their 19-year-old son Morris Jr. and 17-year-old daughter Lisa. Morris has two other children by a former marriage—James, age 26 and Fred, age 30. Morris, age 55, is a professor at Texas Hills University and is in reasonably good health. Over the years he has been able to save and invest a substantial amount of money and now has a personal net worth, including his residence, of approximately $750,000.

---

[1] The term "negotiable" means that the holder of the promissory note may freely sell or transfer the note to somebody else for a portion of its stated value (stated value is the amount owed under the note plus interest). This might be necessary, for example, if the creditor dies and the executor of her estate wants to wind up her affairs and not wait until the borrower pays off the note. See Section D for more on what this term means.

[2] Although we label our notes as being used to borrow or lend money, they may also be used when a debt is created in a different way, as, for example, when payment for an item is deferred to a later time, or a later payment is promised to settle a dispute.

One day Fred calls and asks Morris whether he will lend him $1,500 for three months to buy a computer. Because Fred has always acted responsibly, and since the amount of the loan is not large and the period for its repayment short, Morris says yes and decides not to charge interest or require any formalities other than a simple written note. Accordingly, Morris selects FORM 1: Note to Borrow/Lend Money Repayable in Lump Sum Without Interest.

Shortly after this transaction, James calls and says he and his wife want to borrow $5,000 to remodel their kitchen. Although Morris believes that James tends to be overly optimistic about his ability to repay debts on time, he has total faith in James' wife Joanne. On the condition that James and Joanne both sign the note and agree to pay the loan back within three years, plus simple interest at the rate of 10% per annum, Morris agrees to make the loan, using FORM 2: Note to Borrow/Lend Money Repayable in Lump Sum With Interest.

About this time Morris Jr. decides to buy a car. Although Junior has been thinking along the lines of a new Porsche, Morris Sr. talks him into buying his ten-year-old Mercedes for $8,000 so that he (Morris Sr.) can buy a new one. To finance this arrangement, Junior agrees to pay the $8,000 in equal installments for four years, without interest. Morris Sr. uses FORM 3: Note to Borrow/Lend Money Repayable in Installments Without Interest. If Morris Sr. decided to charge interest, he would use FORM 4: Note to Borrow/Lend Money Repayable in Installments With Interest.

A few months later, James announces he wants to borrow $15,000, repayable in five years, to invest in a small computer-repair store that he and his friends plan to open the following month. After some investigation Morris Sr. decides to loan the money, but because of the amount of the loan and length of time it will take James to repay it, he decides to get James wife's signature on the note and take a security interest (mortgage or deed of trust) in their home as collateral. Accordingly, Morris Sr. uses FORM 5: Note to Borrow/Lend Money Repayable in Lump Sum and Secured by Interest in Real or Personal Property. If James were to pay the note back in installments, Morris Sr. would use FORM 6: Note to Borrow/Lend Money Repayable in Installments and Secured by Interest in Real or Personal Property.

Our sample forms on the following pages show how Morris Sr. would use different promissory notes to make various loans.

D. Some Legal Preliminaries

Before you actually turn to the note that is most appropriate to your situation, you should understand five concepts that are basic to the world of promissory notes. These are:

- attorney fees
- acceleration of installment debts
- negotiability
- joint and several liability and
- co-signing.

Let's briefly review each.

1. Attorney Fees

Unless they agree otherwise, each party to a contract is usually expected to pay his own attorney fees should court enforcement prove necessary. As a practical matter this often means that a note is unenforceable unless the amount due is small and can be recovered in small claims court (or its equivalent) or is large enough to justify paying an attorney. Given the costs and delays inherent in our court system, medium-sized notes usually cost more to collect than their face value. To remedy this situation, we include a provision in all our notes which requires the signer of the note to pay the holder's reasonable attorney fees should the holder prevail in a court action to collect on the note. If you find this clause objectionable, simply cross it out and have the borrower place her initials next to it. (See Chapter 1, Section C(4).)

2. Acceleration of Installment Debt

If you use one of our installment notes (NOTES 3, 4 and 6) you will encounter a somewhat harsh-sounding clause that allows the lender to declare the entire debt immediately due and payable in the event the borrower signing the note is late with an installment payment. Called an "acceleration of maturity" clause, it is commonly included in notes providing for installment payments. It allows the note's holder (the lender or someone the lender has transferred the note to) to immediately move to collect the debt in one lawsuit. Otherwise the note holder would have to wait until all of the installments should have been paid (say a year or two down the line) to bring the lawsuit, or would have to file a separate lawsuit for each installment (impractical and too expensive). As with the attorney fees provision, if you wish to delete this clause, follow the instructions in Chapter 1, Section C(4).

3. Negotiability

All of our notes are negotiable—that is, they can be sold. To understand what this means, think of what happens when you write a check. Your check means that you owe the face amount of the check to the person you have made it out to (the payee) and that your bank will pay this debt when the check is presented to it. The original payee of your check can either collect the amount directly or, as is common, endorse the check to someone else. This new owner can then collect the amount from your bank or endorse the check to someone else. In other words, the check can pass freely from person to person (that is, be negotiated) until it is presented to your bank for payment.

Promissory notes can similarly be negotiated, assuming they contain the following provisions and magic words:

- names of the lender and borrower, and borrower's address
- a statement that the debt is payable "to the order of" the lender (promisee)
- a specified principal sum to be paid and the specific rate of interest, if any
- the address where the payments are to be made
- the city where and date when the note is signed; and
- the signature of the debtor (promisor).

All the notes set out in this book contain this basic information. Although we told you in Chapter 1 that you could alter our contracts to your satisfaction, taking out any of these clauses will probably render the note non-negotiable (though still valid).

In fact, it is unlikely that negotiability will be important to very many readers, as most will never transfer their note. However, should one of the parties die, become mentally ill, or otherwise not be able to pay or collect the debt, the fact that the note is negotiable increases the chance it will be paid. Why? Because institutions in the business of purchasing uncollected notes and collecting on them may be willing to buy it. If you alter a note but want to have it remain negotiable, make sure it still contains the elements listed above.

4. Joint and Several Liability

All of our notes provide that joint signers "jointly and severally" promise to pay the debt. This means that each signer is responsible both for half of the debt (that is, "jointly" promises) and the complete debt (that is, "severally promises"). It is common practice to make joint signers of a note jointly liable and severally liable so that if the debt isn't paid on time (there is a default) the person lending the money can sue and collect the whole amount due from either borrower.

5. Co-signing

Commercial lenders often require that a second, credit-worthy party sign a note in addition to the primary borrower, especially when the primary borrower is young or lacks a good credit standing. This has often proved to be a trap into which many well-meaning people have stumbled. Why? Because a co-signer is equally liable with the primary debtor for the entire debt evidenced by the promissory note. Stated differently, when you co-sign a note, you guarantee its payment; if the primary signer doesn't pay, you must.[3] Yet, because the setting in which the co-signer is asked to sign is typically informal, she often does not realize the extent of her obligations under the note.

Because the notes in this book are not intended for use in commercial contexts, none of them contains a provision for a co-signer. If a second person is to sign one of our notes as drafted, he must do so as a primary joint promisor who is jointly and severally liable for the debt. The joint promisor approach is especially recommended when the borrower is married and the lender wants her spouse's name on the note as well. If, however, you decide that your situation does call for a co-signer (rather than a joint promisor) and you fully discuss with the co-signer the fact that by signing he obligates himself to repay the entire debt if the borrower misses even one payment, add the following clause to the note you wish to use:

ENDORSEMENT:

For value received, I unconditionally guarantee payment of this note, with interest if applicable, in accordance with its terms.

Date: ______________________________

Co-signer's Signature ______________________________

Co-signer's Address ______________________________

[3]However, if the terms and conditions of a note are later changed by the parties and the co-signer does not again sign, he is probably off the hook under the law of most states.

NOTE: Before proceeding to the forms, make sure you have read our instructions in Chapter 1, Section C.

FORM 1 NOTE TO BORROW/LEND MONEY REPAYABLE IN LUMP SUM WITHOUT INTEREST

The note that calls for a lump sum payment and no interest is about as basic as you can get. This sort of note is normally used by people with a close personal relationship when the person lending the money is primarily interested in helping out the borrower and expects nothing in return except, eventually, the amount borrowed.

The note contains the following basic provisions:

- identification of the parties
- the face amount of the note, which is simply the amount borrowed
- the date the note must be paid
- the fact that payment shall be to the order of the lender
- the address where payment is to be made
- a joint and several liability clause (for notes signed by more than one person)
- an attorney fees provision
- the signature of the borrower or borrowers
- the addresses of the borrower or borrowers and
- the city where and date when the note is signed.

A sample of FORM 1 follows. We include a blank tear-out version of this note at the end of this chapter.

SAMPLE FORM 1

Morris Sr. loans Fred $1,500 (interest-free) to be repaid in a lump sum in three months.

PROMISSORY NOTE

1. For value received, ☒ I individually ☐ We jointly and severally promise to pay to the order of Morris Jones *(name of person(s) to whom debt is owed)* $ 1,500 on July 1, 19— *(date payment is due)*, at 123 Post St., Austin, Texas *(address where payment is to be made)*.

2. In the event the holder(s) of this note prevail in a lawsuit to collect on it, I/we agree to pay the holder(s)' attorney fees in an amount the court finds to be just and reasonable.

April 1, 19—	
Date	Date
Austin, Texas	
Location (City or County)	Location (City or County)
Fred Jones	
Name of Borrower	Name of Second Borrower
456 Main St., Dallas	
Address of Borrower	Address of Second Borrower
Fred Jones	
Signature of Borrower	Signature of Second Borrower

FORM 2 NOTE TO BORROW/LEND MONEY REPAYABLE IN LUMP SUM WITH INTEREST

This note is the same as FORM 1, except that simple (non-compounded) interest is provided for. This note is normally used when:

1. The lender does not wish to forgo the interest he would otherwise earn, or

2. A large sum of money is to be lent and the lender wishes to avoid payment of the federal gift tax, which is imposed on gifts of more than $10,000 ($20,000 for a married couple) made within a one-year period. This concept is important because when money is loaned for no interest or at a nominal rate of interest, the difference between the amount of interest charged and a "reasonable"[4] rate of interest is considered to be a gift. Thus, if the interest you forgo by charging less than the reasonable rate is worth more than $10,000, you must file a federal gift tax return.

[4]The IRS actually uses the term "safe harbor" instead of "reasonable," but they amount to the same thing.

From time to time, the IRS decides what this reasonable rate is. It is usually considerably below what a bank would charge. When banks were charging about 16%, the IRS reasonable rate was 10%. In other words, any personal loan carrying an interest rate of 10% or more did not include a gift. However, if a loan was made with a low interest rate, (say 5%), the difference between the 5% interest rate and the 10% "safe harbor" rate was considered to be a gift. Again, all of this is only significant if a very large loan is made at low interest.

Why charge interest? Charging a friend or family member interest strikes some people as being ungenerous. In our opinion this feeling arises from a misconception as to the function of interest. Think of it this way. Suppose Tom loans Harry $5,000 for a year, interest-free. If Tom had put the money in a savings account, he would have earned the going rate of interest. By giving Harry the money interest-free, Tom ends up paying for the privilege of loaning the money to Harry.

How much interest is appropriate? In an effort to be generous to a relative or friend, many lenders charge interest at somewhat less than the market rate, sometimes as little as they would receive if they put it in the bank for the same period of time. This is still a good deal for the borrower; after all, even if Harry could establish credit with a bank and borrow money from it, he would have to pay a much higher rate of interest than Tom would receive if he put the money in a savings account.

Currently, interest charged for family and personal debts tends to run from 7 to 12%. One warning: each state limits the amount of interest that can be charged for a debt. Charging more than this limit is called usury and is a crime. As long as you don't charge more than about 10%,[5] you don't need to worry about usury laws. But check the law before charging a higher rate. Some states have usury limits below 10%, although in many states the usury rate is much higher.

Assuming you plan to charge a certain rate of interest, your next step is to figure out how to compute it. The method we use for computing interest does not provide for compound interest, unlike most commercial notes. Interest is compounded when it is charged not only on the amount of the unpaid loan or debt (the principal) but on the accrued interest as well. In our experience most people who make loans to friends and family don't want to bother with the intricacies of figuring out compound interest. However, because compound interest results in substantially higher interest payments over the life of a loan, people charging simple interest may want to compensate by asking for a slightly higher rate than they otherwise would.

If you decide to use our simple method of computing interest, take the following steps:

Step 1: When you fill out the promissory note, determine what annual rate of interest you wish to charge.

Step 2: To determine the amount of annual interest which will be due on the loan, multiply the amount of the loan by the annual interest rate. For instance, if the loan is for $4,000, and your annual interest rate is 10%, the annual amount of interest on the loan is $400.

Step 3: Multiply the annual interest amount by the time period of the loan. In our example, if the loan is for one year, your interest would be $400, if the loan is for two years, $800, and so on. That amount will be due when the principal sum is due.

Step 4: If you need to compute the interest for a period of months rather than years, compute the interest for one year, divide by 12, and then multiply the result by the number of months. For example, assume the $4,000 loan is for an 18-month period. Take the annual interest amount ($400), divide by 12 ($33.33) and multiply by 18 ($600).

---

[5]The fact that your friendly credit card or finance company may be charging you upwards of 18% interest on unpaid balances does not change what we say here. Usury laws are riddled with exceptions in favor of large financial and corporate interests.

PREPAYMENT NOTE: What happens if in fact the loan is paid back before it is due? You have two choices:

- You can charge the same interest that you would have had the note not been prepaid. This is not unreasonable, since you committed yourself to being without the amount of the entire loan for the time indicated.
- You can prorate the interest to correspond to the actual period of time the loan was outstanding. Returning to the $4,000 loan example, if you originally figured interest at 10% for two years ($800) but the loan was paid back in 18 months, simply charge the 18-month figure ($600) instead.

After you have thought about this issue and perhaps discussed it with the borrower, choose one of the following boxes, which are contained in FORM 2:

---

2. Simple interest shall be charged on the sum specified in Clause 1 at the rate of ______________ % per year (choose one):

☐ from the date this note was signed until the date it is due or is paid in full, whichever date occurs later.

☐ from the date this note was signed until the date it is paid in full.

The first box requires payment of interest at least for the entire length of the loan, and beyond if payment is late. The second box requires the interest to be charged according to when the loan is actually paid back.

Here is a complete sample of FORM 2. A tear-out version is provided at the end of the chapter.

SAMPLE FORM 2

Morris Sr. loans James and Joanne $5,000 to be repaid in three years at 10% annual interest.

PROMISSORY NOTE

1. For value received, ☐ I individually ☒ We jointly and severally promise to pay to the order of Morris Jones *(name of person(s) to whom debt is owed)* $ 5,000 on August 1, 19— *(date payment is due)*, at 123 Post St., Austin, Texas *(address where payment is to be made)*.

2. Simple interest shall be charged on the sum specified in Clause 1 at the rate of 10 % per year (choose one):

   ☐ from the date this note was signed until the date it is due or is paid in full, whichever date occurs later.

   ☒ from the date this note was signed until the date it is paid in full.

3. In the event the holder(s) of this note prevail in a lawsuit to collect on it, I/we agree to pay the holder(s)' attorney fees in an amount the court finds to be just and reasonable.

August 1, 19—	May 1, 19—
Date	Date
Austin, Texas	Austin, Texas
Location (City or County)	Location (City or County)
James Jones	Joanne Jones
Name of Borrower	Name of Second Borrower
789 Ward St.	789 Ward St.
Address of Borrower	Address of Second Borrower
James Jones	
Signature of Borrower	Signature of Second Borrower

FORM 3 NOTE TO BORROW/LEND MONEY REPAYABLE IN INSTALLMENTS WITHOUT INTEREST

Loans are often repaid in installments rather than all at once. When the parties involved in the transaction are friends, the amount borrowed is relatively small, and the probability of repayment is high, you may want to use an interest-free installment note. A sample of FORM 3 is shown below. A tear-out version is found at the end of this chapter. If you desire to use an installment note with interest, use FORM 4 below.

SAMPLE FORM 3

Morris Sr. loans Morris Jr. $8,000 (interest-free) to be repaid in monthly equal installments over a four-year period.

PROMISSORY NOTE

1. For value received, ☒ I individually ☐ We jointly and severally promise to pay to the order of Morris Jones *(name of person(s) to whom debt is owed)* $ 8,000 at 123 Post St., Austin, Texas *(address where payments are to be made)*.

2. ☒ I individually ☐ We jointly and severally also agree that this note shall be paid in equal installments of $ 166.67 per month, due on the first day of each month, until the principal is paid in full.

3. If any installment payment due under this note is not received by the holder within *(number of days)*[6] days of its due date, the entire amount of unpaid principal shall become immediately due and payable at the option of the holder without prior notice to the signer(s) of this note.

4. In the event the holder(s) of this note prevail(s) in a lawsuit to collect on it, I/we agree to pay the holder(s)' attorney fees in an amount the court finds to be just and reasonable.

August 1, 19–	
Date	Date
Austin, Texas	
Location (City or County)	Location (City or County)
Morris Jones, Jr.	
Name of Borrower	Name of Second Borrower
123 Post St., Austin, Texas	
Address of Borrower	Address of Second Borrower
Morris Jones, Jr.	
Signature of Borrower	Signature of Second Borrower

[6] This can be whatever number of days you agree to (e.g., 5 days, 15 days, etc.).

FORM 4 NOTE TO BORROW/LEND MONEY REPAYABLE IN INSTALLMENTS WITH INTEREST

This note is basically the same as the FORM 3 note except that it provides for interest. Charging interest on an installment loan complicates things a little. This is because as the balance due on the note declines, the amount of interest that is payable declines accordingly. In the commercial world, this sliding scale of interest is commonly calculated (by computer) and reflected in a monthly statement. Or, in the case of consumer loans such as car loans and mortgages, the interest is prefigured according to the period of the loan and added to each monthly payment of principal.

For example, if after your down payment you owe $6,000 on your new car, you will sign a note for this amount payable in installments over a fixed period of time. The interest on $6,000 for the period of the note (say four years) will be computed in advance, taking into account that each payment will diminish the amount of outstanding principal and thus cause the amount of interest to similarly decline. Under this system the principal and interest are repaid over the course of the loan in equal installments that go toward both principal and the interest on the unpaid principal.

To help you use this system in our notes, we provide an easy-to-use chart. Here is how to use it.

Step 1: Determine the length of time the loan will be outstanding (that is, the period between the making of the loan and the date all principal and interest must be paid under the terms of the note).

AMORTIZATION SCHEDULE

PERCENTAGE	NUMBER OF YEARS													
	1	1.5	2	2.5	3	4	5	6	7	8	9	10	15	20
5.0	.0856	.0578	.0439	.0355	.0300	.0230	.0189	.0161	.0141	.0127	.0115	.0106	.0079	.0066
5.5	.0858	.0580	.0441	.0358	.0302	.0233	.0191	.0163	.0144	.0129	.0118	.0109	.0082	.0069
6.0	.0861	.0582	.0443	.0360	.0304	.0235	.0193	.0166	.0146	.0131	.0120	.0111	.0084	.0072
6.5	.0863	.0585	.0445	.0362	.0306	.0237	.0196	.0168	.0148	.0134	.0123	.0114	.0087	.0075
7.0	.0865	.0587	.0448	.0364	.0309	.0239	.0198	.0170	.0151	.0136	.0125	.0116	.0090	.0078
7.5	.0868	.0589	.0450	.0367	.0311	.0242	.0200	.0173	.0153	.0139	.0128	.0119	.0093	.0081
8.0	.0870	.0591	.0452	.0369	.0313	.0244	.0203	.0175	.0156	.0141	.0130	.0121	.0096	.0084
8.5	.0872	.0594	.0455	.0371	.0316	.0246	.0205	.0178	.0158	.0144	.0133	.0124	.0098	.0087
9.0	.0875	.0596	.0457	.0373	.0318	.0249	.0208	.0180	.0161	.0147	.0135	.0127	.0101	.0090
9.5	.0877	.0598	.0459	.0376	.0320	.0251	.0210	.0183	.0163	.0149	.0138	.0129	.0104	.0093
10.0	.0879	.0601	.0461	.0378	.0323	.0254	.0212	.0185	.0166	.0152	.0141	.0132	.0107	.0097
10.5	.0881	.0603	.0464	.0380	.0325	.0256	.0215	.0188	.0169	.0154	.0144	.0135	.0111	.0100
11.0	.0884	.0605	.0466	.0383	.0327	.0258	.0217	.0190	.0171	.0157	.0146	.0138	.0114	.0103
11.5	.0886	.0608	.0468	.0385	.0330	.0261	.0220	.0193	.0174	.0160	.0149	.0141	.0117	.0107
12.0	.0888	.0610	.0471	.0387	.0332	.0263	.0222	.0196	.0177	.0163	.0152	.0143	.0120	.0110

Step 2: Determine what basic rate of interest you wish to charge. Interest for family and personal debts tends to run from 7 to 10%. If you wish to charge a higher rate of interest, check your state law to see if it is legal; it may constitute the crime of usury.

Step 3: On the "Amortization Schedule for Monthly Payments"

a. Find your rate of interest in the left-hand column.

b. Find the period of time the loan will be outstanding at the top of the chart.

c. Find the figure where the two columns intersect. For example, if your interest rate is 10% and the loan will be outstanding for five years, the figure at the intersection point is 0.0212.

Step 4: Determine your monthly payment amount (principal and interest).

Multiply the figure found at the intersection of the two columns by the total amount of your loan. The product is your monthly payment. For instance, continuing our example from the last step and assuming a principal of $10,000, multiply 0.0212 by $10,000 to get the monthly payment amount for a $10,000 loan payable in five years ($212). Easy.

What happens if the borrower decides to pay off the principal sooner than the note calls for under the installment plan? Because the interest on each payment assumes the loan will be outstanding for five years, a prepayment renders this assumption false and means that the interest charged during the earlier period of the loan was higher than it should have been.

In commercial contexts, there is a formula under which a borrower can recapture some of this interest. In the personal contracting context we think it unnecessary to compute the amount of credit the signer should receive. Due to the relatively modest amounts which are likely to be involved, it should be possible for the parties to reach a satisfactory agreement to lower the total amount paid at the time the loan is repaid. However, if a lot of money is involved, you may want to consult a banker or accountant to help you figure out a fair recapture amount.

NOTE: Lenders often keep track of the payments made under an installment note to avoid disputes over whether any particular payment was made. To help you with this task, we provide you with a monthly payment record (FORM 7), a tear-out version of which is at the end of this chapter. Simply follow the instructions at the top of the form.

Here is a sample of FORM 4. A tear-out version is located at the end of the chapter.

SAMPLE FORM 4

Morris Sr. loans Morris Jr. $8,000 to be repaid in monthly equal installments at 10% annual interest over a four-year period.

PROMISSORY NOTE

1. For value received, ☒ I individually ☐ We jointly and severally promise to pay to the order of Morris Jones *(name of person(s) to whom debt is owed)* $ 8,000 at 123 Post St., Austin, Texas *(address where payment is to be made)* with interest at the rate of 10 % per year (choose one):

   ☐ from the date this note is signed until the date it is due or is paid in full, whichever date occurs last.[7]

   ☒ from the date this note was signed until the date it is paid in full.[8]

2. ☒ individually ☐ We jointly and severally also agree that this note shall be paid in installments, which include principal and interest, of not less than $ 203.20 per month, due on the first day of each month, until such time as the principal and interest are paid in full.

3. If any installment payment due under this note is not received by the holder within *(choose number of days)*[9] days of its due date, the entire amount of unpaid principal shall become immediately due and payable at the option of the holder without prior notice to the signer(s) of this note.

4. In the event the holder(s) of this note prevail(s) in a lawsuit to collect on it, I/we agree to pay the holder(s)' attorney fees in an amount the court finds to be just and reasonable.

August 1, 19—	
Date	Date
Austin, Texas	
Location (City or County)	Location (City or County)
Morris Jones, Jr.	
Name of Borrower	Name of Second Borrower
123 Post St., Austin, Texas	
Address of Borrower	Address of Second Borrower
Morris Jones, Jr.	
Signature of Borrower	Signature of Second Borrower

[7]This option does not allow credit for prepayment.

[8]This option allows credit for prepayment.

[9]This can be whatever number of days you agree to (e.g., 5 days, 15 days, etc.)

FORM 5 FORM 6 NOTES TO BORROW/LEND MONEY SECURED BY INTERESTS IN REAL OR PERSONAL PROPERTY

These notes are the same as those discussed above except that they refer to a separate agreement or document by which property belonging to the borrower is specified as collateral for repayment of the loan. In our earlier example, Morris Sr. agrees to loan James $15,000 to invest in a computer repair store but wants James' house to be security (collateral) for repayment of the loan. If this contract is written correctly, and James fails to repay the amount when due, Morris Sr. would legally own the house and could obtain possession of it in a court action if necessary.

Unfortunately, specifying that property of the borrower is collateral for the loan is not as easy as it might seem. Although most consumer protection laws don't apply to non-commercial transactions, a few do. For instance, in most states, to legally establish property as collateral for a loan, a special agreement (called a "security agreement") must be signed by the borrower in addition to the promissory note. And usually the security agreement must be recorded with a public agency (called "perfecting" the security interest) as a condition of claiming the property ahead of other creditors, should the borrower default. Telling you how to do this in your state is beyond the scope of this book. However, if you know someone who routinely deals with installment sales of any kind, the chances are this person can help you.

Further, if real estate is involved it is usually necessary for the debtor to sign and have notarized[10] a mortgage deed (called a deed of trust in some states) putting title to the property in the hands of a third party until the loan is paid off.[11] The deed should then be recorded with the county recorder; if it isn't, and the debtor sells the property to someone else, the creditor may find that his ownership of the property has been wiped out. Mortgage deeds are available at most office supply stores and are not difficult to fill out. If you need help, anyone in the real estate business should be able to provide it.[12]

Assuming you are able to properly execute a mortgage deed, deed of trust or security agreement for personal property, FORM 5 should be used if your loan is repayable in a lump sum, and FORM 6 if your loan is repayable in installments. A sample of the provision tying the promissory note to the security interest or mortgage (deed of trust) is shown below. Tear-out versions of FORM 5 and FORM 6 are located at the end of this chapter.

[10]In this situation it might be a good idea to have the note notarized as well as the deed. To do this, hunt up a notary public from a bank or real estate office, sign the note in her presence, have her stamp and sign the note, and pay the $5-$10 it costs to have this done.

[11]If money is already owed on the property, the debtor would execute a second or even third mortgage or deed of trust.

[12]If the real estate is in California, you can use Nolo's *Deeds Book*, by Mary Randolph, to accomplish this task.

SECURED INTEREST PROVISION

☐ I individually ☐ We jointly and severally agree that until such time as the principal and interest owed under this note are paid in full, the note shall be secured by the following described mortgage, deed of trust or security agreement: ____________________

____

____

____

Sample Descriptions

House as Security:

"Deed of trust to real property commonly known as *(address or other description)*, owned by *(name)* executed on *(date signed)* at *(place signed)* and recorded at *(place recorded)* in the records of ________ County, *(State)*."

Car as Security:

"Security agreement signed by *(name)* on *(date)* which gives ________ title to a 1982 Dodge Dart, I.D. # ________."

Coin Collection as Security:

"Security agreement signed by ________ on *(date)* which gives ________ a security interest in promisor's collection of 128 pre-1900 United States coins listed on Attachment 1."

PROMISSORY NOTE

LOAN REPAYABLE IN LUMP SUM WITHOUT INTEREST

1. For value received, ☐ I individually ☐ We jointly and severally promise to pay to the order of ____________________

   ____ $ ______________________________

   on ______________________________, at ____

   ____

2. In the event the holder(s) of this note prevail(s) in a lawsuit to collect on it, I/we agree to pay the holder(s)' attorney fees in an amount the court finds to be just and reasonable.

____
Date

____
Location (City or County)

____
Name of Borrower

____
Address of Borrower

____

____
Signature of Borrower

____
Date

____
Location (City or County)

____
Name of Second Borrower

____
Address of Second Borrower

____

____
Signature of Second Borrower

PROMISSORY NOTE

LOAN REPAYABLE IN LUMP SUM WITH INTEREST

1. For value received, ☐ I individually ☐ We jointly and severally promise to pay to the order of ____________________

   ____ $ ____________________

   on ____________________________, at ____

   ____

2. Simple interest shall be charged on the sum specified in Clause 1 at the rate of ________ % per year (choose one):

   ☐ from the date this note was signed until the date it is due or is paid in full, whichever date occurs later.

   ☐ from the date this note was signed until the date it is paid in full.

3. In the event the holder(s) of this note prevail(s) in a lawsuit to collect on it, I/we agree to pay the holder(s)' attorney fees in an amount the court finds to be just and reasonable.

______________________ Date	______________________ Date
______________________ Location (City or County)	______________________ Location (City or County)
______________________ Name of Borrower	______________________ Name of Second Borrower
______________________ Address of Borrower	______________________ Address of Second Borrower
______________________	______________________
______________________ Signature of Borrower	______________________ Signature of Second Borrower

PROMISSORY NOTE

LOAN REPAYABLE IN INSTALLMENTS WITHOUT INTEREST

1. For value received, ☐ I individually ☐ We jointly and severally promise to pay to the order of ______________________

   ____ $ ______________________________

   at ____

   ____

2. ☐ I individually ☐ We jointly and severally also agree that this note shall be paid in equal installments of $__________

   per month, due on the first day of each month, until the principal is paid in full.

3. If any installment payment due under this note is not received by the holder within ______________ days of its due date, the entire amount of unpaid principal shall become immediately due and payable at the option of the holder without prior notice to the signer(s) of this note.

4. In the event the holder(s) of this note prevail(s) in a lawsuit to collect on it, I/we agree to pay the holder(s)' attorney fees in an amount the court finds to be just and reasonable.

______________________________ Date	______________________________ Date
______________________________ Location (City or County)	______________________________ Location (City or County)
______________________________ Name of Borrower	______________________________ Name of Second Borrower
______________________________ Address of Borrower ______________________________	______________________________ Address of Second Borrower ______________________________
______________________________ Signature of Borrower	______________________________ Signature of Second Borrower

PROMISSORY NOTE

LOAN REPAYABLE IN INSTALLMENTS WITH INTEREST

1. For value received, ☐ I individually ☐ We jointly and severally promise to pay to the order of ______________________

   ____ $ __________________________________

   at ____

   ____

   at the rate of %____________________ per year (choose one):

   ☐ from the date this note was signed until the date it is due or is paid in full, whichever date occurs last.

   ☐ from the date this note was signed until the date it is paid in full.

2. ☐ I individually ☐ We jointly and severally also agree that this note shall be paid in installments, which include principal and interest, of not less than $_________________ per month, due on the first day of each month, until such time as the principal and interest are paid in full.

3. If any installment payment due under this note is not received by the holder within _______________________ days of its due date, the entire amount of unpaid principal shall become immediately due and payable at the option of the holder without prior notice to the signer(s) of this note.

4. In the event the holder(s) of this note prevail(s) in a lawsuit to collect on it, I/we agree to pay the holder(s)' attorney fees in an amount the court finds to be just and reasonable.

_______________________________	_______________________________
Date	Date
_______________________________	_______________________________
Location (City or County)	Location (City or County)
_______________________________	_______________________________
Name of Borrower	Name of Second Borrower
_______________________________	_______________________________
Address of Borrower	Address of Second Borrower
_______________________________	_______________________________
_______________________________	_______________________________
Signature of Borrower	Signature of Second Borrower

PROMISSORY NOTE

LOAN REPAYABLE IN LUMP SUM AND SECURED BY INTEREST IN REAL OR PERSONAL PROPERTY

1. For value received, ☐ I individually ☐ We jointly and severally promise to pay to the order of ______________________

   ____ $ ______________________

   on ______________________, at ______________________________________

   ____

2. Simple interest shall be charged on the sum specified in Clause 1 at the rate of __________ % per year (choose one):

   ☐ from the date this note was signed until the date it is due or is paid in full, whichever date occurs later.

   ☐ from the date this note was signed until the date it is paid in full.

3. In the event the holder(s) of this note prevail(s) in a lawsuit to collect on it, I/we agree to pay the holder(s)' attorney fees in an amount the court finds to be just and reasonable.

4. ☐ I individually ☐ We jointly and severally agree that until such time as the principal and interest owed under this note are paid in full, the note shall be secured by the following described mortgage, deed of trust, or security agreement:

   ____

   ____

   ____

   ____

______________________ Date	______________________ Date
______________________ Location (City or County)	______________________ Location (City or County)
______________________ Name of Borrower	______________________ Name of Second Borrower
______________________ Address of Borrower	______________________ Address of Second Borrower
______________________	______________________
______________________ Signature of Borrower	______________________ Signature of Second Borrower

PROMISSORY NOTE

LOAN REPAYABLE IN INSTALLMENTS AND SECURED BY INTEREST IN REAL OR PERSONAL PROPERTY

1. For value received, ☐ I individually ☐ We jointly and severally promise to pay to the order of ____________________

   ____ $ ____________________

   on ______________________________, at ____

   ____

   at the rate of %____________________ per year (choose one):

   ☐ from the date this note was signed until the date it is due or is paid in full, whichever date occurs last.

   ☐ from the date this note was signed until the date it is paid in full.

2. ☐ I individually ☐ We jointly and severally also agree that this note shall be paid in installments, which include principal and interest, of not less than $__________________ per month, due on the first day of each month, until such time as the principal and interest are paid in full.

3. If any installment payment due under this note is not received by the holder within ____________________ days of its due date, the entire amount of unpaid principal shall become immediately due and payable at the option of the holder without prior notice to the signer(s) of this note.

4. In the event the holder(s) of this note prevail(s) in a lawsuit to collect on it, I/we agree to pay the holder(s)' attorney fees in an amount the court finds to be just and reasonable.

5. ☐ I individually ☐ We jointly and severally agree that until such time as the principal and interest owed under this note are paid in full, the note shall be secured by the following described mortgage, deed of trust, or security agreement:

   ____

   ____

   ____

______________________________	______________________________
Date	Date
______________________________	______________________________
Location (City or County)	Location (City or County)
______________________________	______________________________
Name of Borrower	Name of Second Borrower
______________________________	______________________________
Address of Borrower	Address of Second Borrower
______________________________	______________________________
______________________________	______________________________
Signature of Borrower	Signature of Second Borrower

MONTHLY PAYMENT RECORD

Month	(A) Beginning Balance (Prior Month Ending Balance)	(B) Interest Rate Divided by 12	(C) Interest Due (A) x (B)	(D) Payment	(E) Principal Reduction (D) — (C)	(F) Ending Balance (A) — (E)
1						
2						
3						
4						
5						
6						
7						
8						
9						
10						
11						
12						
13						
14						
15						
16						
17						
18						
19						
20						
21						
22						
23						
24						

Chapter 3

Bills of Sale

This chapter contains forms for use in private sales of personal property such as cars, boats, appliances, furniture and computers. Indeed, these simple bills of sale are designed to be used to record the terms of sale of all types of property, with the exception of real estate and items such as securities, stocks and commercial paper, the sale of which is closely regulated by law.

A. Why Bills of Sale Are Useful

Buying and selling is the lifeblood of many if not most of the world's cultures. Ours is no exception. The great bulk of sales involve groceries, over-the-counter drugs, restaurant meals, liquor, clothing and other relatively inexpensive consumer items. These transactions occur in a reasonably informal context. While it's true that the great majority produce receipts, most of us tend promptly to throw them away.

There are, however, many situations where more formal documentation of the terms of a sale can be extremely helpful if not downright necessary. Sales of motor vehicles, boats, jewelry, art works, stereo equipment, machinery, furniture, furs, appliances, computers and other expensive items are always accompanied by a written "bill of sale" when purchased new. This provides a means of proving ownership and the terms of the sale, and is often essential should a purchaser have a problem with the item and try to return it.

In addition, when valuable items are involved, a buyer may be called on to establish ownership of property when it is registered, insured or sold, or (in unusual situations) in response to police queries. The bill of sale often serves as "title" to the object, at least where no other evidence of title has been established by law, as it has, for example, for motor vehicles, real property and securities. Jewelry, paintings, furs, electronic equipment and collections of all types are prime examples of valuable property that tend to be bought and sold without the passing of a written, formal "title." In these situations, bills of sale are crucial.

Bills of sale also provide sellers an invaluable opportunity to fully and honestly disclose the condition of the goods, whether inspections have been made, etc. Doing this is an excellent way for a seller to protect himself in advance from a buyer who is attacked by "buyer's remorse" soon after his purchase and is looking for a way to back out of the sale.

As stated, businesses that sell goods usually provide their own bills of sale. On the other hand, sellers who are not in business (that is, who engage in an occasional private sale) and who are selling items which are used rather than new are normally not equipped with the necessary documents. The forms in this chapter are designed to remedy this problem.

B. What Is In a Bill of Sale?

A bill of sale is a written document which at a minimum includes:

- a statement that the sale has taken place;
- a description of the item sold;
- a statement of the amount paid; and
- the signature of the person selling the property and the date.

In addition, bills of sale often include:

- a promise by the seller that he has the right to sell the item;
- warranties (legally binding guarantees) or disclaimers of any warranties; and
- disclosures of any major defects known to the seller.

In the belief that all sales should take place in an open atmosphere of full disclosure, we include these additional provisions in all of our bills of sale. In addition, we provide a space for the buyer to sign. Although the buyer's signature is not needed to carry out most of the objectives of the bill of sale, as described earlier, it can be very useful should the buyer later disagree with statements in it.

C. Bills of Sale in This Chapter

This chapter contains four bills of sale:

FORM 1: General bill of sale for transactions involving such miscellaneous personal property as furniture, appliances, electronic equipment, pets, tools, collections or art works.

FORM 2: Bill of sale for motor vehicles, including cars, trucks, motorcycles, recreational vehicles and movable mobile homes.

FORM 3: Bill of sale for computer system, useful when all or most of an entire computer system is being sold.

FORM 4: Bill of sale for boat, for all kinds of recreational and personal seacraft.

After several additional introductory sections, we briefly discuss each of these bills of sale in the next few pages. At the end of the chapter you will find tear-out versions of each.

D. Forms of Joint Ownership

Our forms are designed for use by individual or joint buyers. When there are two buyers, both their names go on the bill of sale and both are asked to sign. This is all that the seller needs. However, this is not the end of the matter for the buyers. They will have to decide among themselves on the form of their joint ownership. If your situation involves only an individual buyer, skip to Section E.

There are several different ways of jointly owning property. The owners can be tenants in common, joint tenants, tenants by the entirety (a form of joint tenancy for married couples) or own the property as community property (if they are married and live in certain states). Let's take a moment to define these terms.

Tenants in Common: When two or more persons own property as tenants in common, each owns a share of the entire property. Whether these shares are equal or unequal depends on what the people agree to among themselves. This agreement need not be reflected in the bill of sale. The share owned by each tenant is her separate property, which can be sold or willed to others and which will be inherited by the person's heirs if there is no will. In other words, if one tenant in common dies, the others do not automatically inherit her share.

If the owners do not make an agreement to the contrary, the property is assumed to be owned in equal shares by the owners as tenants in common.

Joint Tenancy with Right of Survivorship: When two or more people own property as joint tenants with right of survivorship, each owns an equal share of the entire property. Each owner may transfer his share to another person (this is easier in some states than in others) but this automatically destroys the joint tenancy and transforms it into a tenancy in common. Most important, under joint tenancy with right of survivorship, each owner's share does not pass to his beneficiaries or heirs at death but instead passes to the other joint tenants. In some states (but not the community property states listed below), property held jointly by a married couple as "husband and wife" may be treated as a type of joint tenancy called a "tenancy by the entirety."

Community Property: In California, Nevada, Arizona, New Mexico, Idaho, Texas, Louisiana, Washington and Wisconsin, most property acquired by a couple in the course of their marriage is considered "community property" (owned equally by the spouses), unless the parties specifically agree to a different form of ownership. This usually means that neither spouse may dispose of the property without the consent of the other, and that the property is divided between the spouses (or their estates) in the event of death or divorce.

Which of these forms of joint ownership is best? The answer obviously depends on the context and desires of the buyers.

For certain types of property (for example, automobiles, boats or mobile homes) the form of ownership can be designated on the certificate of title form provided by the state licensing agency. For property that doesn't carry a certificate of title, however, the joint buyers should execute a separate agreement between themselves specifying the form of ownership. The following contract can be used for this purpose. A tear-out version is located at the end of this chapter.

JOINT OWNERSHIP AGREEMENT

1. We, ______________________________ and ______________________________, are joint buyers of the property specified in the bill of sale executed on ____________________, a copy of which is attached to this Agreement.

2. We agree that this property shall be owned by us as(choose one):

☐ tenants in common in equal shares.

☐ tenants in common in the following percentages:

(describe the percentages of ownership) ______________________________.

☐ joint tenants with right of survivorship.

☐ tenants by the entirety.

☐ community property.

Signed ______________________________ Dated: ____________________

Signed ______________________________ Dated: ____________________

E. Warranties

When a seller of goods or services makes an express representation about her wares (for example, "This works perfectly," "I fixed the transmission at a cost of $1,000 last week," or "This motorbike is guaranteed for normal use for 30 days") or guarantees that the goods or services will work for a particular period of time, she has made an express warranty. Express warranties can be delivered either orally or in writing. Warranties of three months or more are common for new goods; used goods are rarely warranted for more than 30 days, if at all.

In addition to express warranties, a seller of new goods is deemed to make certain implied warranties (that is, the law considers them implied in the contract even though they aren't written out). One of these, called the "warranty of merchantability," is that the goods are fit for their generally intended use. If you sell a used item, the warranty of merchantability is a promise that the product will work as expected, given its age and condition. If a used refrigerator cools down to 45 degrees without any problem (cold enough so that food won't spoil), but the door sticks or the light flashes every so often, this isn't a breach of the warrant of merchantability.

Another implied warranty—the implied warranty of fitness—is that the goods are fit for the specific (even unusual) use intended by the buyer if the seller knows the intended use.

If the seller offers an express warranty for any period of time (for example, 30 days), she is usually deemed to offer the implied warranties at least for the same length of time. On the other hand, if no express warranty is made and the goods are sold "as is," the seller may in most states legally disclaim these implied warranties (that is, tell the buyer that they don't apply) as long as it's done clearly. Also, in most states, these implied warranties apply only to new goods. In designing our bills of sale we had two major considerations. One was that most sellers of used goods desire that the sale be final. This generally means that no express warranties are made and that all implied warranties are disclaimed. The second is that buyers of used goods expect to be informed of defects which are known to the seller. To accommodate both considerations we have drafted our forms so that they:

- disclaim implied warranties in all states where such disclaimers are allowed[1]
- provide a space for the seller to disclose all known major defects in the property and
- (for cars and boats) provide for incorporation of an inspection report into the bill of sale.

If the seller wants to provide a warranty, she should cross out the disclaimer language and insert the terms of the warranty, for example, "Property warranted to work properly for 30 days." See Chapter 1, Section C(4) for how to make these changes.

NOTE: The form of our notes obviously reflects our biases. If you disagree with our full disclosure approach, you may delete this clause in the manner suggested in Chapter 1.

For information on state laws regarding warranties, contact your State Consumer Protection Office (see the list in the Appendix).

F. Selling Property Partially Owned By Others

Each of our bills of sale requires the seller to state if anyone else owns all or part of the item being sold. For instance, if the seller has pledged his household furniture as collateral for a bank loan and decides to sell the furniture using one of our bills of sale, the fact that the bank has an ownership interest (commonly called a lien) must be disclosed to the buyer. Claims such as liens that others have on your property are called encumbrances. What effect does this disclosure have on the sale? Simply that the buyer is put on notice that the other owner's permission may be necessary for the sale to be valid. And because, realistically, permission is usually contingent upon the other owner being paid some money, our forms also contain a clause in which the seller commits to making this payment.

NOTE: Before proceeding to the forms, read our instructions in Chapter 1 on how to fill them in.

FORM 1 GENERAL BILL OF SALE FOR MISCELLANEOUS PERSONAL PROPERTY

This form should be used for items which don't fall into one of the other categories specifically covered in this chapter. Examples of items for which this form is appropriate are jewelry, art works, sports equipment, rare books, furniture, collections, appliances, tools, photographic equipment and electronic items. A filled-in sample form follows. A tear-out version of this form is located at the end of the chapter.

---

[1] If you live in any of the following states, and if the goods you are selling are covered by an implied warranty (unusual for used goods), your disclaimer may not be upheld if it ever becomes an issue: Mississippi, Massachusetts, West Virginia, Kansas, Maryland, Vermont and Maine.

SAMPLE FORM 1

PERSONAL PROPERTY BILL OF SALE

1. *(Name(s) of seller(s))*, Seller(s), hereby sell(s) the goods described in paragraph 2 to *(Name(s) of buyer(s))*, Buyer(s).

2. The goods being sold under this bill of sale (Goods) are: *(describe the goods in sufficient detail to uniquely identify them)*
______
______

> *Examples:*
>
> *a. Jewelry:* "7/8 ct Diamond/Ruby cocktail ring, yellow gold, purchased from Dudly Diamonds, S.F., 1978."
>
> *b. Coin collection:* "120 U.S. coins from 1879 to 1986 (most in "fine" condition), including 1896 quarter minted in Denver, 1910 Liberty nickel minted in Philadelphia, etc."
>
> *c. Sports equipment:* "190 cm Rossignol header skies, poles and Nordica ski boots, 1984 model."
>
> *d. Musical Instrument:* "Steinway baby grand piano, Serial #____."

3. The full purchase price for Goods is $______. In exchange for Goods, Buyer(s) has/have paid Seller(s) (choose one):

☐ the full purchase price.

☐ $______ as a down payment, balance due in ______ days.

☐ $______ as a down payment and has/have executed a promissory note[2] for the balance of the purchase price.

4. Seller(s) warrant(s) that Seller(s) is/are the legal owner(s) of Goods and that Goods are free of all liens and encumbrances except *(put any ownership interest claimed by others)*.

Seller(s) agree(s) to remove any lien or encumbrance specified in this clause with the proceeds of this sale within ______ days of the date of the bill of sale.

---

[2]In this situation, the buyer would execute one of the promissory notes in Chapter 2.

5. Seller(s) believe(s) Goods to be in good condition except for the following: *(describe any important defects in Goods which are known to seller)*

6. Other than the warranty of ownership in Clause 4 and the representations in Clause 5, seller(s) make(s) no express warranties. **The Buyer(s) take(s) all goods as is.** Seller(s) hereby disclaim(s) the implied warranty of merchantability and all other implied warranties which may apply to the extent that such disclaimers are permitted in the state having jurisdiction over this bill of sale.

7. Goods shall be delivered to Buyer(s) in the following manner (choose one and fill in information if Box b or c is checked):

☐ a. Buyer shall take immediate possession of Goods.

☐ b. Buyer(s) assume(s) responsibility for picking up goods from *(location)* within ________ days.

☐ c. In exchange for an additional delivery charge of $____________, receipt of which is hereby acknowledged, Seller(s) will deliver Goods within ________ days to the following location: ____________________

8. Additional terms of sale for Goods are as follows: *(describe additional important terms not covered by other provisions)*

Date Seller(s) Signed

Signature of Seller

Address of Seller

Signature of Seller

Address of Seller

Date Buyer(s) Signed

Signature of Buyer

Signature of Buyer

FORM 2 BILL OF SALE FOR MOTOR VEHICLE (CAR, MOTORCYCLE, MOTORHOME)

This bill of sale is for vehicles that must be registered with your state's Department of Motor Vehicles. This typically includes cars, trucks, motorcycles, recreational vehicles and mobile homes that are truly mobile. It does not include stationary non-registered mobile homes that are designed to be used semi-permanently at a fixed location such as a mobile home park. Such homes are commonly treated as real property—just as if they were houses—and as such are covered by special transfer, financing and recording rules not discussed here. The category of motor vehicle also doesn't include off-road farm machinery (use FORM 1 instead) unless it is registrable in your state as a motor vehicle.

The clauses in this form are straightforward. The vehicle should be described in detail. The price paid for it is included in case a Department of Motor Vehicles wants this information to compute a sales or use tax. The seller represents that she has the right to sell the vehicle.[3] And a general disclaimer of warranties is included to protect the seller against later claims by the buyer that the vehicle didn't measure up to the seller's representations or the buyer's expectations. A space for the car's odometer reading is also provided. Contact your State Consumer Protection Office (see Appendix) for any special requirements when selling a used motor vehicle.[4]

In this regard, the bill of sale requires the seller to disclose any major defects known to her, and also allows the seller to indicate whether or not the vehicle has been subjected by the buyer to an independent mechanical inspection. Inspection is common and advised for the protection of all parties, since it is virtually impossible to accurately assess the condition of a used vehicle just by looking at it. If an inspection has been made, the parties are given the option of including the inspection report as part of the bill of sale. Our recommendation is that you do so, since the more disclosures there are on the bill of sale, the less the parties will have to argue about should the vehicle fail after the sale.

The following is a sample of this bill of sale. A tear-out version is located at the end of this chapter.

[3]Most motor vehicles come with a certificate of ownership which is physically transferred from the seller to the buyer. This is normally adequate proof of ownership. If, for some reason, such evidence is missing, the buyer would be wise to check the seller's claims of ownership with the state agency handling motor vehicle registrations.

[4]In California, for example, certain safety features must be working on the used car: horn, lights, windshield wipers, tires and brakes. Also, the smog equipment must be intact. And sellers of used cars must provide buyers with an original smog certificate that is no more than 90 days old.

SAMPLE FORM 2

MOTOR VEHICLE BILL OF SALE

1. *(Name(s) of seller(s))*, Seller(s), hereby sell(s) and deliver(s) the vehicle described in Clause 2 to *(Name(s) of buyer(s))*, Buyer(s).

2. The vehicle being sold under this bill of sale (Vehicle) is a *(year and make)*. Its body type is *(motorhome, van, R.V., four-door sedan, two-door coupe, convertible, pickup truck etc.)*. It carries the following I.D., serial or Engine No.:____________________. Vehicle includes the following personal property items: *(tools, luggage rack, radio tape deck, car cover, etc.)*.

3. The full purchase price for Vehicle is $______________. In exchange for Vehicle, Buyer(s) has/have paid Seller(s) (choose one):

   ☐ the full purchase price.

   ☐ $__________________ as a down payment, balance due in __________ days.

   ☐ $__________________ as a down payment and has executed a promissory note[5] for the balance of the purchase price.

4. Seller(s) hereby warrant(s) that Seller(s) is/are the legal owner(s) of Vehicle and that Vehicle is free of all liens and encumbrances except *(put any claims of ownership by others to Vehicle if known)*

   ____

   ____

   Seller(s) agree(s) to remove any lien or encumbrance specified in this clause with the proceeds of this sale within ten days of the date of this bill of sale.

5. Vehicle (choose one) ☐ has been ☐ has not been inspected by an independent mechanic at buyer's request.

   If an inspection has been made, the inspection report (choose one) ☐ is attached ☐ is not attached to and made part of this bill of sale.

---

[5] In this situation, the buyer would execute one of the promissory notes contained in Chapter 2.

6. Seller(s) believe(s) Vehicle is in good condition except for the following defects: *(describe all known major defects)* ______________________

____

____

7. Other than the warranty of ownership in Clause 4 and the representations in Clause 6, Seller(s) make(s) no express warranties. **The Buyer(s) take(s) vehicle as is.** Seller(s) hereby disclaim(s) the implied warranty of merchantability and all other implied warranties which may apply to the extent disclaimers are permitted in the state having jurisdiction over this bill of sale.

8. The odometer reading for Vehicle is: ______________________

9. Additional terms of sale for Vehicle are as follows: *(describe additional important terms not covered by other provisions)*

____

____
Date Seller(s) Signed

____
Signature of Seller

____
Address of Seller

____

____

____
Signature of Seller

____
Address of Seller

____

____

____
Date Buyer(s) Signed

____
Signature of Buyer

____
Signature of Buyer

FORM 3 BILL OF SALE FOR COMPUTER SYSTEM

This bill of sale should be used for computers, computer peripherals and software, especially where a whole system is being sold. If only one or two components are being sold, FORM 1 should be adequate. A filled-in sample of FORM 3 follows. A tear-out version is located at the end of this chapter.

SAMPLE FORM 3

COMPUTER SYSTEM BILL OF SALE

1. *(Name(s) of seller(s))*, Seller(s), hereby sell(s) and deliver(s) the goods described in Clause 2 to *(Name(s) of buyer(s))*, Buyer(s).

2. The goods being sold under this bill of sale (Goods) are: (choose one or more)

☐ A computer (boards, cpu, bus, I/O ports) carrying the brand name of ______ and the following serial number:______.

☐ The following monitors:

#1: *(brand)* *(serial number)*

#2: *(brand)* *(serial number)*

#3: *(brand)* *(serial number)*

☐ One or more floppy disk drives carrying the brand name of ______ and the following serial number: ______.

☐ One or more hard disk drives carrying the brand name of ______ and the following serial number: ______.

☐ One or more mass storage devices carrying the brand name of ______ and the following serial number: ______.

☐ One or more CD-ROM devices carrying the brand name of ______ and the following serial number: ______.

☐ The following printers:

#1: *(brand)* *(serial number)*

#2: *(brand)* *(serial number)*

☐ A modem carrying the brand name of ______ and the following serial number: ______.

☐ Computer-related furniture or other items as follows: *(describe other equipment, such as third printer, printer stand, muffler box for printer, special cables)*.

☐ Software consisting of the following:

Title	Serial No.
______	______
______	______

(refer to attachment for additional software)[6] ______________________

3. The full purchase price for Goods is $ ______________. In exchange for Goods, Buyer(s) has/have paid Seller(s) (choose one):

   ☐ The full purchase price.

   ☐ $______________ as a down payment, balance due in ______________ days.

   ☐ $______________ as a down payment and has/have executed a promissory note[7] for the balance of the purchase price.

4. Seller(s) hereby warrant(s) that Seller(s) is/are the legal owner or licensee of Goods and that Goods are free of all liens and encumbrances except *(list any claims by other parties to equipment)*. Seller(s) agree(s) to remove any lien or encumbrance specified in this clause with the proceeds of this sale within ten days of the date Seller(s) signs this bill of sale.

5. Seller(s) believe(s) Goods to be in good condition except for the following defects: *(describe major defects known to Seller(s))*.

6. Other than the warranty of ownership in Clause 4 and the representations in Clause 5, Seller(s) make(s) no express warranties. **The Buyer(s) take(s) all goods as is.** Seller(s) hereby disclaim(s) the implied warranty of merchantability and all other implied warranties which may apply to the extent such disclaimers are permitted in the state having jurisdiction over this bill of sale.

7. Additional terms of sale for Goods are as follows: *(describe additional important terms not covered by other provisions)*.

______________________ ______________________
Date Seller(s) Signed Date Buyer(s) Signed

______________________ ______________________
Signature of Seller Signature of Buyer

____
Address of Seller

______________________ ______________________
 Signature of Buyer

____

____
Signature of Seller

____
Address of Seller

____

____

[6] If you need more room to describe the software (or anything else) being sold, see the instructions in Chapter 1, Section C(6).

[7] In this situation, the buyer would execute one of the promissory notes contained in Chapter 2.

FORM 4 BILL OF SALE FOR BOAT

This form is similar in content to the bill of sale for a motor vehicle (FORM 2) but includes some special entries for items unique to boat sales. A sample of FORM 4 is shown below. A tear-out version of this form is located at the end of this chapter.

SAMPLE FORM 4

BOAT BILL OF SALE

1. *(Name(s) of seller(s)* ____________, Seller(s), hereby sell(s) and deliver(s) the boat described in Clause 2 to *(Name(s) of buyer(s)* ____________, Buyer(s).

2. The boat being sold under this bill of sale (Boat) is described as follows:

   Year: ________ Make: ____________ Model: ________

   Length: ____________ Serial No. : ____________

   Registration Number: ____________

   General type: *(for example, sailboat, cabin cruiser, etc.)* ____________

3. Boat has: (check one) ☐ no engine ☐ one engine ☐ two engines ☐ an auxiliary engine.

4. The engine(s) (Engines) are described as follows:

   a. Engine No. 1 is described as follows:

      Year: ____________ Make: ____________

      Type: ____________ Serial No: ____________

   b. Engine No. 2 is described as follows:

      Year: ____________ Make: ____________

      Type: ____________ Serial No: ____________

   c. The auxiliary engine is described as follows:

      Year: ____________ Make: ____________

      Type: ____________ Serial No: ____________

5. Boat contains the following equipment (Equipment) (check one or more and describe):

   ☐ a. Sails: ____________________

   ☐ b. Bilge pump: ____________________

   ☐ c. Ship to Shore radio: ____________________

   ☐ d. Radar: ____________________

   ☐ e. Sonar: ____________________

   ☐ f. Other: *(describe all additional removable or extra items which come with the boat, such as galley equipment, dinghy, fishing gear, life vests, deck furniture, etc.)*.

6. Seller(s) believe(s) Boat, Engines and Equipment to be in good condition except for the following defects: *(describe known major defects)*

7. Boat and Engines (check one) ☐ have been ☐ have not been independently inspected at Buyer's request. The inspection report (choose one) ☐ is attached ☐ is not attached to and made part of this bill of sale.

8. The full purchase price for Boat, Engines and Equipment is $ ____________. In exchange for Boat, Engines and Equipment Buyer(s) has/have paid Seller(s) (choose one):

   ☐ the full purchase price.

   ☐ $ ____________ as a down payment, balance due in ____________ days.

   ☐ $ ____________ as a down payment and has executed a promissory note[8] for the balance of the purchase price.

---

[8] In this situation, the buyer would execute one of the promissory notes contained in Chapter 2.

9. Seller(s) warrant(s) that Seller(s) is/are the legal owner(s) of Boat, Engines and Equipment and that Boat, Engines and Equipment are free of all liens and encumbrances except: *(describe claims of ownership by third parties which you know of)*.

   Seller(s) agree(s) to remove any lien or encumbrance specified in this clause with the proceeds of this sale within ten days after the date of this bill of sale.

10. Other than the warranty of ownership in Clause 9 and the representations in Clause 6, Seller(s) make(s) no express warranties. **The Buyer(s) take(s) boats, engines and equipment as is.** Seller(s) hereby disclaim(s) the implied warranty of merchantability and all other implied warranties which may apply to the extent that such disclaimers are permitted in the state having jurisdiction over this bill of sale.

11. Additional terms of sale for Boat, Engines and Equipment are as follows: *(describe additional important terms not covered by other provisions)*

____

Date Seller(s) Signed

Signature of Seller

Address of Seller

____

____

Signature of Seller

Address of Seller

____

____

Date Buyer(s) Signed

Signature of Buyer

Signature of Buyer

JOINT OWNERSHIP AGREEMENT

1. We, ____

   and ____, are joint

   buyers of the property specified in the bill of sale executed on ____________________, a copy of which is

   attached to this Agreement.

2. We agree that this property shall be owned by us as (choose one):

   ☐ tenants in common in equal shares.

   ☐ tenants in common in the following percentages:

   ____.

   ☐ joint tenants with right of survivorship.

   ☐ tenants by the entirety.

   ☐ community property.

Signed: ____________________________________ Dated: ____________________

Signed: ____________________________________ Dated: ____________________

PERSONAL PROPERTY BILL OF SALE

1. ____, Seller(s), hereby sell(s) the goods described in paragraph 2 to ____, Buyer(s).

2. The goods being sold under this bill of sale (Goods) are: ____
____
____
____

3. The full purchase price for Goods is $______________. In exchange for Goods, Buyer(s) has/have paid Seller(s) (choose one):

☐ the full purchase price.

☐ $________________ as a down payment, balance due in ______________ days.

☐ $________________ as a down payment and has/have executed a promissory note for the balance of the purchase price.

4. Seller(s) warrant(s) that Seller(s) is/are the legal owner(s) of Goods and that Goods are free of all liens and encumbrances except
____.

Seller(s) agree(s) to remove any lien or encumbrance specified in this clause with the proceeds of this sale within ________ days of the date of the bill of sale.

5. Seller(s) believe(s) Goods to be in good condition except for the following defects: ______________________________
____
____

6. Other than the warranty of ownership in Clause 4 and the representations in Clause 5, seller(s) make(s) no express warranties. **The Buyer(s) take(s) all goods as is.** Seller(s) hereby disclaim(s) the implied warranty of merchantability and all other implied warranties which may apply to the extent that such disclaimers are permitted in the state having jurisdiction over this bill of sale.

7. Goods shall be delivered to Buyer(s) in the following manner (choose one and fill in information if Box b or c is checked):

☐ a. Buyer shall take immediate possession of Goods.

☐ b. Buyer(s) assume(s) responsibility for picking up goods from __________________________ within ________ days.

☐ c. In exchange for an additional delivery charge of $ ____________, receipt of which is hereby acknowledged, Seller(s) will deliver Goods within ________ days to the following location: ______________________________

8. Additional terms of sale for Goods are as follows: ____
____
____.

Date Seller(s) Signed

Date Buyer(s) Signed

Signature of Seller

Signature of Buyer

Address of Seller

Signature of Buyer

Signature of Seller

Address of Seller

MOTOR VEHICLE BILL OF SALE

1. ______________________________, Seller(s), hereby sell(s) and deliver(s) the vehicle described in Clause 2 to ______________________________, Buyer(s).

2. The vehicle being sold under this bill of sale (Vehicle) is a ______________________________. Its body type is ______________________________. It carries the following I.D., serial or Engine No.:______________________________. Vehicle includes the following personal property items: ______________________________.

3. The full purchase price for Vehicle is $ __________. In exchange for Vehicle, Buyer(s) has/have paid Seller(s) (choose one):

   ☐ the full purchase price.

   ☐ $__________ as a down payment, balance due in __________ days.

   ☐ $__________ as a down payment and has executed a promissory note for the balance of the purchase price.

4. Seller(s) hereby warrant(s) that Seller(s) is/are the legal owner(s) of Vehicle and that Vehicle is free of all liens and encumbrances except: ______________________________
____
______________________________.

   Seller(s) agree(s) to remove any lien or encumbrance specified in this clause with the proceeds of this sale within ten days of the date of this bill of sale.

5. Vehicle (choose one) ☐ has been ☐ has not been inspected by an independent mechanic at buyer's request.

   If an inspection has been made, the inspection report (choose one) ☐ is attached ☐ is not attached to and made part of this bill of sale.

6. Seller(s) believe(s) Vehicle is in good condition except for the following defects: ______________________________
____
____
______________________________.

7. Other than the warranty of ownership in Clause 4 and the representations in Clause 6, Seller(s) make(s) no express warranties. **The Buyer(s) take(s) vehicle as is.** Seller(s) hereby disclaim(s) the implied warranty of merchantability and all other implied warranties which may apply to the extent disclaimers are permitted in the state having jurisdiction over this bill of sale.

8. The odometer reading for Vehicle is: ______________________________

9. Additional terms of sale for Vehicle are as follows: ______________________________

____

____

Date Seller(s) Signed	Date Buyer(s) Signed
Signature of Seller	Signature of Buyer
Address of Seller	
	Signature of Buyer

Signature of Seller

Address of Seller

COMPUTER SYSTEM BILL OF SALE

1. ______________________________, Seller(s), hereby sell(s) and deliver(s) the goods described in Clause 2 to ______________________________, Buyer(s).

2. The goods being sold under this bill of sale (Goods) are: (choose one or more)

☐ A computer (boards, cpu, bus, I/O ports) carrying the brand name of ______________________________ and the following serial number: ______________________________.

☐ The following monitors:

#1: ______________________________ ______________________________

#2: ______________________________ ______________________________

#3: ______________________________ ______________________________

☐ One or more floppy disk drives carrying the brand name of ______________________________ and the following serial number: ______________________________.

☐ One or more hard disk drives carrying the brand name of ______________________________ and the following serial number: ______________________________.

☐ One or more mass storage devices carrying the brand name of ______________________________ and the following serial number: ______________________________.

☐ One or more CD-ROM devices carrying the brand name of ______________________________ and the following serial number: ______________________________.

☐ The following printers:

#1: ______________________________ ______________________________

#2: ______________________________ ______________________________

☐ A modem carrying the brand name of ______________________________ and the following serial number: ______________________________.

☐ Computer-related furniture or other items as follows: ______________________________

____

______________________________.

☐ Software consisting of the following:

Title:	Serial No.:
______________________________	______________________________
______________________________	______________________________
______________________________	______________________________
______________________________	______________________________
______________________________	______________________________

3. The full purchase price for Goods is $_______________. In exchange for Goods, Buyer(s) has/have paid Seller(s) (choose one):

☐ The full purchase price.

☐ $_______________ as a down payment, balance due in _______ days.

☐ $_______________ as a down payment and has/have executed a promissory note for the balance of the purchase price.

4. Seller(s) hereby warrant(s) that Seller(s) is/are the legal owner or licensee of Goods and that Goods are free of all liens and encumbrances except ____

____

____. Seller(s) agree(s) to remove any lien or encumbrance specified in this clause with the proceeds of this sale within ten days of the date Seller(s) signs this bill of sale.

5. Seller(s) believe(s) Goods to be in good condition except for the following defects: ______________________________

____

____

____.

6. Other than the warranty of ownership in Clause 4 and the representations in Clause 5, Seller(s) make(s) no express warranties. **The Buyer(s) take(s) all goods as is.** Seller(s) hereby disclaim(s) the implied warranty of merchantability and all other implied warranties which may apply to the extent such disclaimers are permitted in the state having jurisdiction over this bill of sale.

7. Additional terms of sale for Goods are as follows: ______________________________

____

____.

____
Date Seller(s) Signed

____
Signature of Seller

____
Address of Seller

____

____

____
Signature of Seller

____
Address of Seller

____

____

____
Date Buyer(s) Signed

____
Signature of Buyer

____
Signature of Buyer

BOAT BILL OF SALE

1. ______________________________, Seller(s), hereby sell(s) and deliver(s) the boat described in Clause 2 to ______________________________, Buyer(s).

2. The boat being sold under this bill of sale (Boat) is described as follows:

   Year: __________ Make: ____________________ Model: __________

   Length: ______________ Serial No. ______________

   Registration Number: ______________________________

   General type: ______________________________

3. Boat has: (check one) ☐ no engine ☐ one engine ☐ two engines ☐ an auxiliary engine.

4. The engine(s) (Engines) are described as follows:

   a. Engine No. 1 is described as follows:

      Year: __________ Make: ______________________

      Type: __________ Serial No: ______________________

   b. Engine No. 2 is described as follows:

      Year: __________ Make: ______________________

      Type: __________ Serial No: ______________________

   c. The auxiliary engine is described as follows:

      Year: __________ Make: ______________________

      Type: __________ Serial No: ______________________

5. Boat contains the following equipment (Equipment) (check one or more and describe):

   ☐ a. Sails: ______________________________

   ____

   ☐ b. Bilge pump: ______________________________

   ____

   ☐ c. Ship to Shore radio: ______________________________

   ____

   ☐ d. Radar: ______________________________

   ____

   ☐ e. Sonar: ______________________________

   ____

   ☐ f. Other: ______________________________

   ____

6. Seller(s) believe(s) Boat, Engines, and Equipment to be in good condition except for the following defects: ____________________

____.

7. Boat and Engines (check one) ☐ have been ☐ have not been independently inspected at Buyer's request. The inspection report (choose one) ☐ is attached ☐ is not attached to and made part of this bill of sale.

8. The full purchase price for Boat, Engines and Equipment is $____________________. In exchange for Boat, Engines and Equipment Buyer(s) has/have paid Seller(s) (choose one):

☐ the full purchase price.

☐ $____________________ as a down payment, balance due in ______________ days.

☐ $____________________ as a down payment and has executed a promissory note for the balance of the purchase price.

9. Seller(s) warrant(s) that Seller(s) is/are the legal owner(s) of Boat, Engines and Equipment and that Boat, Engines and Equipment are free of all liens and encumbrances except: ____

____

____

____.

Seller(s) agree(s) to remove any lien or encumbrance specified in this clause with the proceeds of this sale within ten days after the date of this bill of sale.

10. Other than the warranty of ownership in Clause 9 and the representations in Clause 6, Seller(s) make(s) no express warranties. **The Buyer(s) take(s) boats, engines and equipment as is.** Seller(s) hereby disclaim(s) the implied warranty of merchantability and all other implied warranties which may apply to the extent that such disclaimers are permitted in the state having jurisdiction over this bill of sale.

11. Additional terms of sale for Boat, Engines, and Equipment are as follows: ______________________________

____

____.

____
Date Seller(s) Signed

____
Signature of Seller

____
Address of Seller

____

____

____
Signature of Seller

____
Address of Seller

____

____

____
Date Buyer(s) Signed

____
Signature of Buyer

____
Signature of Buyer

Chapter 4

Contracts Governing Storage of Goods

It is common to store property—everything from bikes and beds to washing machines and motorcycles—with friends and relatives. Sometimes this amounts to leaving a few small objects for a short time. On other occasions, it means storing a house or garage full of goods for a year or more. In many situations involving friends and family, money isn't charged for storage, although it is certainly appropriate to do so when bulky or valuable objects are stored for a considerable period of time. This is especially true when the goods are stored in a place (for example, a garage or spare room) that might otherwise be rented.

Especially when a fee is charged for storage, but even when it isn't, it is a good idea to commit some mutual understandings to paper to make sure that everyone understands who's responsible should the stored property suffer harm. Otherwise the property owner generally ends up absorbing any loss that occurs if the goods are damaged or stolen, even if it was the result of carelessness on the part of the person storing the property. Surely, if a problem occurs, having a simple written storage contract will enhance efforts to arrive at a fair settlement and help preserve relations between the parties.

This chapter provides several basic agreements that can be used when property is stored. As with the other chapters, the agreements are intended for personal (as opposed to commercial) use. The features of each contract are briefly noted at the beginning of each section.

A. Some Terminology Defined

When an owner of property places it in someone else's temporary possession, the legal name for the transaction is a "bailment." In law, the owner of the property being stored is called the bailor while the person storing the property is called the bailee. Maybe you never realized that you were entering into such a gobbledygook-filled legal transaction when you asked your parents to store your books, but there you have it. You never know when a little law is going to sneak into your life. In our contracts, we use the term "Owner" to refer to the "bailor" (the person whose property is being stored) and the term "Bailee" for the person who is providing the storage. The fact that we use only one bit of legal jargon ("Bailee") should help you tell one party from the other when you are filling in the contracts.

B. The Contracts in This Chapter

The contracts provided in this chapter cover a range of storage needs. Briefly, they consist of the following:

FORM 1: Simple storage contract under which bailee does not receive payment and assumes no responsibility for property.

FORM 2: Simple storage contract providing for storage of the property for an indefinite period (which may be terminated on notice), payment of bailee, exercise of reasonable care for the property by bailee and a dispute resolution provision.

FORM 3: Formal storage contract providing for a fixed term of storage which can only be terminated by notice, payment of bailee, exercise by bailee of reasonable care toward the property, a method for resolving disputes and a requirement that the goods be stored at a specific location.

FORM 4: Formal storage contract providing for an open-ended term of storage, payment of bailee, a duty to exercise reasonable care by the bailee, a method for resolving disputes and a requirement that the goods stored be kept at a specific location.

FORM 5: Formal storage contract providing an open-ended storage period for payment of the bailee, a requirement that the goods stored be kept at a specific location, mandatory insurance provided by the bailee, absolute responsibility of bailee to return the property in the same condition and a method for resolving disputes.

FORM 6: Contract for boarding of animals.

C. Example of How Contracts in This Chapter Are Used

Barbara and Wayne have been married for twenty-five years and have lived in the same house in the same city for most of that time. They have three adult children. Barbara is a creative consultant for several publishing firms and Wayne is a professor at one of the local colleges. One day Wayne receives an offer from a colleague in Paris who offers him a visiting professorship at the Sorbonne, to begin in six months. Wayne accepts, which means both he and Barbara must focus considerable energy on planning for their year abroad.

They lease the house to Phil, a junior faculty member at the college, for the year, but because Phil has three small children they decide to store much of their valuable personal property elsewhere. Wayne's best friend Bob agrees to care for Wayne's valuable collection of 1930's records, his sporting equipment and a half-dozen power tools. Barbara's good friend Mary agrees to store the clothes that Barbara and Wayne will not be taking with them. Because payment for these favors is out of the question between close friends, Wayne and Barbara use the simple bailment contract contained in FORM 1, discussed below. Why use a contract at all? By writing down their mutual expectations, the friends go a long way towards avoiding the possibility of misunderstandings should something happen to the property.

INSURANCE NOTE: It is no secret that Americans, as a people, have covered themselves with wall-to-wall insurance when possible. Accordingly, virtually all homeowners purchase homeowner's insurance policies which provide coverage for the house, their household possessions and liability to others that results from their status as a property owner. Approximately 25% of renters carry a roughly equivalent renter's insurance.

These policies usually provide protection not only for property owned by the homeowner (or renter) but also property that they have rightful possession of, even though it belongs to someone else. However, it is highly advisable, and even required under some policies, that the owner of the property and the insured (under the homeowner's policy) have a written storage agreement. Under this simple form, Bob and Mary are not formally liable to Wayne and Barbara in case something happens to the property. However, assuming Bob and Mary store the property at their homes under a written agreement, their homeowner's or renter's policies will cover the goods should an insurable loss, such as fire or theft, occur. If Bob and Mary do rely on their homeowner's policies in this context, they should check to see that their policy limits can accommodate the value of the additional property. If not, they may have to extend this coverage for an extra fee (which undoubtedly would be picked up by Wayne and Barbara).

Wayne arranges to store his heavy-duty woodworking equipment (lathe, saw, drill press, router) with Frank, a colleague at the college who he knows and likes, but who is not a close personal friend. Although Wayne trusts Frank to look out for the equipment, he wants a more formal arrangement than he has with his friend Bob. He therefore offers to pay Frank $100 to store the equipment for the year. In exchange, Frank agrees to exercise reasonable care to assure that the equipment is not damaged or stolen while he has it. FORM 3 (discussed in more detail below) is appropriate for this agreement. If Frank was going to store the equipment for an indefinite rather than a fixed period, Wayne would more sensibly use FORM 2 (discussed below) because it anticipates a continuous storage term that can be ended by the bailee at any time.

INSURANCE NOTE: If Frank stored the equipment at his home, it might be covered by his homeowner's or renter's insurance policy as discussed above (assuming the policy limits could accomodate it)—except for losses from floods or earthquakes, unless special coverage is purchased. However, because Frank receives money under this agreement in exchange for storing the property, some homeowner's policies might consider the storage a business transaction and deny coverage on that ground. Even if the homeowner's or renter's policy did extend to the stored equipment, an endorsement (special specific coverage) might be in order. If Frank stored the equipment somewhere other than his home, his normal homeowner's insurance would definitely not cover it, and an added endorsement would clearly be indicated. For this reason, the agreement provides for an extra charge in case Frank must pay for an endorsement to his policy or to raise the coverage limits to accommodate the added value of the equipment. If you are concerned about insurance coverage for stored property, call your broker.

Wayne decides to store his two-year-old BMW with a local garage where he takes the car to be repaired. Because the car is quite valuable, Wayne definitely wants a formal written agreement with the mechanic. The mechanic of course expects payment for the storage.[1] If the mechanic agrees to be absolutely responsible for any damage or theft, the contract set out in FORM 5 (discussed in more detail below) would be appropriate. If, on the other hand, the mechanic only agrees to exercise reasonable care (for example, he is only liable for damage caused by his negligence), Wayne should use FORM 4.

Wayne and Barbara own two animals, a dog and a horse. A neighbor agrees to care for the dog in exchange for prepayment of the animal's expected upkeep costs. The horse is boarded out with a friend who has a few acres in the country. FORM 6 is used for these transactions.

[1] If the mechanic were in the storage business he would probably have his own storage (bailment) contract.

NOTE: Before proceeding to the forms, carefully read Chapter 1 for instructions.

FORM 1 SIMPLE STORAGE CONTRACT UNDER WHICH BAILEE DOES NOT RECEIVE FEES AND ASSUMES NO RESPONSIBILITY FOR PROPERTY

This contract is intended for informal storage situations where the property is not of great value, and the person who will care for the property is a relative or friend of the person who owns it. Here is a sample of FORM 1. A tear-out version is located at the end of this chapter.

SAMPLE FORM 1

STORAGE CONTRACT

1. *(Owner of the property being stored)*, Owner, desires to store the following property (Property): *(describe property being stored)*.

2. *(Person with whom Property is being stored)*, Bailee, agrees to accept and store Property for Owner.

3. Property shall be stored at the following location: *(address where Property is being stored)*.

4. Bailee shall return Property to Owner at any time that either party desires.[2]

5. The parties recognize that Bailee is not being directly compensated for his or her services. Bailee shall not be held liable to Owner for any damage to or theft of Property, no matter what the cause.[3]

6. Any provision in this contract found to be invalid shall have no effect on the validity of the remaining provisions.[4]

7. Additional terms for the storage of Property under this contract are as follows: *(describe additional terms not covered by other provisions)*.

Date	Date
Signature	Signature
Address	Address

[2]This clause gives the bailee the right to return the property at any time. If you want a commitment that the bailee will keep the property for a set time, use FORM 3.

[3]This clause makes it clear that the storage is an act of friendship and that the owner assumes all risk. However, as we stated in our discussion of FORM 1, the bailee's homeowner's or renter's insurance policy may cover loss or damage to the property stored.

[4]If a particular clause of the contract is deemed by a court to be unenforceable for some reason, this clause acts to keep the rest of the contract in effect. Without this clause it is possible that the entire contract would be considered invalid, depending on how important the unenforceable clause was to the entire agreement.

FORM 2 **SIMPLE STORAGE CONTRACT PROVIDING STORAGE OF THE PROPERTY FOR AN INDEFINITE PERIOD (WHICH MAY BE TERMINATED ON NOTICE) FOR PAYMENT OF BAILEE, EXERCISE OF REASONABLE CARE FOR THE PROPERTY BY BAILEE AND A DISPUTE RESOLUTION PROVISION**

This contract is more formal than the one in FORM 1, in that it calls for payment, obligates the bailee to use reasonable care, and has provisions to deal with termination of the storage and dispute resolution. It should be used when the property being stored is valuable or when the additional clauses are desired by either of the parties. A filled-in sample follows, and a tear-out version of FORM 2 is at the back of the chapter.

SAMPLE FORM 2

STORAGE CONTRACT

1. *(Owner of property being stored)*, Owner, desires to store the following property (Property): *(describe property being stored)*.

2. *(Person with whom property is being stored)*, Bailee, agrees to store this property on a *(daily, weekly, monthly, annual)* basis in exchange for payment of $ *(storage fee)* per *(day, week, month, year)*, payable on the first day of each such period.

3. The storage shall commence on *(first day of storage)* and shall continue until Owner claims the property or Bailee serves a written ______ day notice terminating this storage agreement. If Owner claims the property in the middle of a period for which payment has been made, no prorata refund shall be made.

4. Property shall be stored at the following location: *(address where Property is being stored)* ______.

5. Owner and Bailee agree that the approximate (check one)[5] ☐ replacement value ☐ fair market value of each item of Property on the date this agreement is signed is: $ *(specify the value of each item described under Clause 1)*.

[5]It is important to agree on the value of stored property in case it is destroyed or stolen. The value of property can be measured by what a sale in the open marketplace would bring (its fair market value), or what it would cost the owner to replace it (its replacement value). For many items such as collectibles (art, stamps, coins, classic cars, etc.), and property that normally depreciates in value over time, the replacement value will often be higher than the fair market value. For many other items, fair market value is a good way to measure the loss. Our contracts allow you to select either method of valuation. However, keep this in mind: If the contract requires the bailee of property to exercise due care, as most of ours do, the bailee will have to pay up to the amount indicated in this space should he fail in this obligation.

6. Property being stored appears to be in good condition except for the following defects or damage:[6] ____________________ ____.

7. Bailee shall exercise reasonable care to protect Property from theft or damage. Responsibility for theft and damage to Property that doesn't result from the Bailee's negligence shall be borne by Owner.[7]

8. If any dispute arises under the terms of this agreement, the parties agree to select a mutually agreeable neutral third party to help them mediate it.[8] If the mediation is deemed unsuccessful, the parties agree that (choose one):

☐ the dispute shall be decided by the applicable small claims court (or its equivalent)[9] if the amount in dispute is within the court's jurisdiction, and otherwise by binding arbitration under the rules issued by the American Arbitration Association. The decision of the arbitrator shall be final.

☐ the dispute shall be directly submitted to binding arbitration under the rules issued by the American Arbitration Association. The decision of the arbitrator shall be final.[10]

---

[6]When property owned by one person is placed in the hands of another, it is very important for the parties to agree on the property's condition. Months or years down the road the owner of the property will tend to remember it as being in excellent condition whereas the possessor will remember its obvious and plentiful defects. The point of this clause is to prevent such painful misunderstandings.

[7]Reasonable care is the type of care that a reasonable person would exercise under the circumstances. Negligence is the failure to exercise this care. The question of when reasonable care has or has not been exercised must be determined on a case by case basis. The failure by parties to agree on this question is one of the primary reasons so many lawsuits are filed. To avoid this result, our agreements all encourage mediation and out-of-court settlement paths.

[8]Mediation is a process whereby two disputing parties meet with a neutral third party in an effort to settle the dispute. The mediator has no power to impose a decision, only to try to help the parties arrive at one. If the parties agree, a settlement contract is drawn up and everyone, if not happy, is at least minimally satisfied. If no agreement can be reached, then the parties may proceed to one of the other indicated remedies. Incidentally, there is no way to force a party to mediate under this clause. On the other hand, the clause does allow the parties to initially agree on the best way to approach any dispute which happens to arise.

[9]This clause requires the parties to take their dispute to small claims court (or a comparable court if your state doesn't have a "small claims court" as such) if mediation fails and the money in dispute is within the court's jurisdictional limit (usually between $500 and $5,000). Small claims court is the cheapest and easiest way to resolve minor disputes involving money. The procedures can be handled without an attorney, and many small claims courts bar attorneys from representing the litigants. Under this clause, if your dispute involves amounts which are higher than the small claims court has authority to handle, you are required to submit the dispute to an arbitrator as described in note 8 just below.

[10]An arbitrator acts like a judge (only far more informally) and decides the matter for you. Arbitration is an increasingly popular method for solving disputes that can't be solved by mediation. The arbitration process is private—that is, it must be paid for. However, it is still considerably cheaper and faster than the courts. There are either one or three arbitrators, depending on the desires of the parties. The parties can select their own arbitrator or arbitrators, if there is someone they agree on, or apply to an organization that provides arbitrators (such as the American Arbitration Association) for assistance. Under these contracts, the arbitration is governed by American Arbitration Association rules, which specify everything from the time when arbitration must commence to the format for the hearing and the rendering of the decision. The arbitrator's

☐ the dispute shall be settled according to the laws of the state that apply to this agreement.[11]

Any costs and fees (other than attorney fees) associated with mediation and arbitration shall be shared equally by the parties.

9. Attorney fees associated with arbitration or litigation shall be paid as follows (choose one):[12]

☐ Each party shall pay his or her own attorney fees.

☐ The reasonable attorney fees of the prevailing party shall be paid by the other party.

10. All agreements between the parties related to the storage of Property are incorporated in this contract. Any modification to this contract shall be in writing.[13]

11. Any provision in this contract found to be invalid shall have no affect on the validity of the remaining provisions.[14]

12. Additional terms for the storage of Property under this contract are as follows: *(describe additional terms not covered by other provisions)*.

Date	Date
Signature	Signature
Address	Address

decision is final: each party is bound by it and cannot obtain a review in court. Thus, if you definitely think you will want a court to review the dispute somewhere down the line, don't select this option.

[11]Under this remedy, either party is free to seek whatever legal relief is available (usually a court action) under the laws of the state governing the contract (almost always the state in which it is signed). While on the one hand this remedy gives the parties flexibility, on the other it denies them access to the relatively inexpensive and speedy dispute resolution process of arbitration. They may (unless they choose small claims court) have to deal with the formalities of the judicial system, which are almost uniformly formidable and often require the services of an attorney. Court delays of two years or more are not uncommon, and costs (including attorney fees) are often higher than the amount at stake. Unless you feel strongly that you wish to preserve your court "remedies," we recommend you choose either of the previous two options (small claims court or arbitration).

[12]The parties can determine in advance how attorneys who are used in the arbitration of court procedures will be paid. It is the general rule that each side pays its own. However, our forms allow the parties to alter this practice and provide that the winner has her reasonable attorney fees paid by the other party. The decision maker (arbitrator or judge) determines what amount is reasonable.

[13]This clause is fairly standard in written contracts. First, it expressly states that any agreements the parties have reached about the subject matter of the contract are contained in the contract. Second, it provides that all modifications to the contract must be in writing. Together, these provisions prevent a party from later claiming that additional oral or written promises were made but just not included in the written agreement.

[14]If a particular clause of the contract is deemed by a court to be unenforceable for some reason, this clause acts to keep the rest of the contract in effect. Without this clause it is possible that the entire contract would be considered invalid, depending on how important the unenforceable clause was to the entire agreement.

FORM 3 **FORMAL STORAGE CONTRACT PROVIDING A FIXED TERM OF STORAGE WHICH CAN ONLY BE TERMINATED BY NOTICE, PAYMENT OF BAILEE, EXERCISE BY BAILEE OF REASONABLE CARE TOWARD THE PROPERTY, A METHOD FOR RESOLVING DISPUTES AND A REQUIREMENT THAT THE GOODS BE STORED AT A SPECIFIC LOCATION**

This contract should be used when the property is to be stored at a specific location for a definite time and the owner wants to rely on the bailee to keep the property for the duration. For example, if Joss plans to go abroad for a year and arranges to store her furniture with her neighbor Tim, she wants to be sure Tim will take care of the property for the entire year. A sample of this contract follows. A tear-out version of FORM 3 is located at the end of the chapter.

SAMPLE FORM 3

STORAGE CONTRACT

1. *(Owner of property being stored)*, Owner, desires to store the following property (Property): *(describe property being stored)*.

2. *(Person with whom property is being stored),* Bailee, agrees to store Property for payment by Owner of $ ______________. Payment shall be made on or before ______________.

3. The storage shall commence on *(first day of storage)* and continue until *(last day of storage)*, or until Owner claims Property, whichever occurs first.

4. If Owner fails to claim Property on or before the last day of storage indicated in Clause 3, Bailee shall continue to store Property at the rate of $ ________ per *(day, week, month or year)* until Property is claimed or Bailee provides Owner with a ________ day written notice that the storage is being terminated and that Property will be sold if not claimed prior to the date specified in the notice.

5. If Owner fails to claim Property before the period specified in Clause 4 expires, Property shall be deemed abandoned. Bailee shall then sell Property, apply the proceeds to outstanding storage fees and hold the balance for Owner.

6. If Property is claimed by Owner during any period for which payment has already been made, no prorata refund shall be made.

7. Property shall be stored at the following location: *(address where property is being stored)*. Property shall not be removed from this location without prior written notice to and written consent of Owner.

8. Owner and Bailee agree that the approximate (check one)[15] ☐ replacement value ☐ fair market value of each item of Property on the date this agreement is signed is: $ *(specify the value of each item described under Clause #1)* .

9. Property being stored appears to be in good condition except for the following defects or damage:[16] *(describe any major defects)* .

10. Bailee shall exercise reasonable care to protect Property from theft or damage. Responsibility for theft and damage to Property that doesn't result from Bailee's negligence shall be borne by the Owner.[17]

11. If any dispute arises under the terms of this agreement, the parties agree to select a mutually agreeable neutral third party to help them mediate it.[18] If the mediation is deemed unsuccessful, the parties agree that (choose one):

    ☐ the dispute shall be decided by the applicable small claims court (or its equivalent)[19] if the amount in dispute is within the court's jurisdiction, and otherwise by binding arbitration under the rules issued by the American Arbitration Association. The decision of the arbitrator shall be final.

    ☐ the dispute shall be directly submitted to binding arbitration under the rules issued by the American Arbitration Association. The decision of the arbitrator shall be final.[20]

    ☐ the dispute shall be settled according to the laws of the state that apply to this agreement.[21]

    Any costs and fees (other than attorney fees) associated with mediation and arbitration shall be shared equally by the parties.

12. Attorney fees associated with arbitration or litigation shall be paid as follows (choose one):[22]

    ☐ Each party shall pay his or her own attorney fees.

    ☐ The reasonable attorney fees of the prevailing party shall be paid by the other party.

13. All agreements between the parties related to storage of Property are incorporated in this contract. Any modification of the contract shall be in writing.[23]

---

[15]See footnote 5, Sample Form 2.

[16]See footnote 6, Sample Form 2.

[17]See footnote 7, Sample Form 2.

[18]See footnote 8, Sample Form 2.

[19]See footnote 9, Sample Form 2.

[20]See footnote 10, Sample Form 2.

[21]See footnote 11, Sample Form 2.

[22]See footnote 12, Sample Form 2.

[23]See footnote 13, Sample Form 2.

14. Any provision in this contract found to be invalid shall have no affect on the validity of the remaining provisions.[24]

15. Additional terms for the storage of Property under this contract are as follows: *(describe additional terms not covered by other provisions)*.

Date	Date
Signature	Signature
Address	Address

This agreement is similar to FORM 3, but does not bind the bailee for a definite period of time.

[24] See footnote 14, Sample Form 2.

SAMPLE FORM 4

STORAGE CONTRACT

1. *(Owner of property being stored)*, Owner, desires to store the following property (Property): *(describe property being stored)*.

2. *(Person with whom property is being stored)*, Bailee, agrees to store Property on a *(daily, weekly, monthly, annual)* basis in exchange for payment of $ *(storage fee)* per *(day, week, month or year)* payable on the first day of each such period.

3. The storage shall commence on *(first day of storage)* and shall continue until Owner claims Property or Bailee serves a ________ day written notice on Owner terminating this storage agreement. If Owner fails to claim Property on or before the last day of storage indicated in this notice, Bailee may (choose one):

   ☐ continue to store Property at the rate of $ ________ per *(day, week, month or year)* until Property is claimed.

   ☐ deem Property to be abandoned, sell it to pay for outstanding storage fees and hold the balance for Owner.

4. If Owner claims Property during the period for which payment has been made, no prorata refund shall be made.

5. Bailee shall not deliver Property to any person other than Owner without prior written permission from the Owner.

6. Property shall be stored at the following location: ________________________________.

   Property shall be stored under physical conditions which are designed to preserve it from damage, injury or theft.

7. Owner and Bailee agree that the approximate (check one)[25] ☐ replacement value ☐ fair market value of each item of Property on the date this agreement is signed is: $ *(specify the value of each item described under Clause #1)*.

8. Property appears to be in good condition except for the following defects or damage:[26] *(describe any major defects)*.

9. Bailee shall exercise reasonable care to protect the property from theft or damage. Responsibility for theft and damage to Property that doesn't result from Bailee's negligence shall be borne by Owner.[27]

10. The title to Property shall remain at all times in Owner.

---

[25]See footnote 5, Sample Form 2.

[26]See footnote 6, Sample Form 2.

[27]See footnote 7, Sample Form 2.

11. If any dispute arises under the terms of this agreement, the parties agree to select a mutually agreeable neutral third party to help them mediate it.[28] If the mediation is deemed unsuccessful, the parties agree that (choose one):

   ☐ the dispute shall be decided by the applicable small claims court (or its equivalent)[29] if the amount in dispute is within the court's jurisdiction, and otherwise by binding arbitration under the rules issued by the American Arbitration Association. The decision of the arbitrator shall be final.

   ☐ the dispute shall be directly submitted to binding arbitration under the rules issued by the American Arbitration Association. The decision of the arbitrator shall be final.[30]

   ☐ the dispute shall be settled according to the laws of the state that apply to this agreement.[31]

   Any costs and fees (other than attorney fees) associated with mediation and arbitration shall be shared equally by the parties.

12. Attorney fees associated with arbitration or litigation shall be paid as follows (choose one):[32]

   ☐ Each party shall pay his or her own attorney fees.

   ☐ The reasonable attorney fees of the prevailing party shall be paid by the other party.

13. All agreements between the parties relating to the storage of Property are incorporated in this contract. Any modifications to this contract shall be made in writing.[33]

14. Any provision in this contract found to be invalid shall have no effect on the validity of the remaining provisions.[34]

15. Additional terms for the storage of Property under this contract are as follows: *(describe additional terms not covered by other provisions)*.

Date	Date
Signature	Signature
Address	Address

[28]See footnote 8, Sample Form 2.

[29]See footnote 9, Sample Form 2.

[30]See footnote 10, Sample Form 2.

[31]See footnote 11, Sample Form 2.

[32]See footnote 12, Sample Form 2.

[33]See footnote 13, Sample Form 2.

[34]See footnote 14, Sample Form 2.

FORM 5 **FORMAL STORAGE CONTRACT PROVIDING AN OPEN-ENDED STORAGE PERIOD, FOR PAYMENT OF THE BAILEE, A REQUIREMENT THAT THE GOODS STORED BE KEPT AT A SPECIFIC LOCATION, MANDATORY INSURANCE PROVIDED BY THE BAILEE, ABSOLUTE RESPONSIBILITY OF BAILEE TO RETURN THE PROPERTY IN THE SAME CONDITION, AND A METHOD FOR RESOLVING DISPUTES**

This contract is useful in a more arm's-length situation where the property being stored is especially valuable. Here the bailee assumes full responsibility for any damage to the property and is required to provide insurance coverage of the property. A sample agreement follows. A tear-out version of FORM 5 is located at the end of the chapter.

SAMPLE FORM 5

STORAGE CONTRACT

1. *(Owner of property being stored)*, Owner, desires to store the following property (Property): *(describe property being stored)*.

2. *(Person with whom property is being stored)*, Bailee, agrees to store Property on a *(daily, weekly, monthly or yearly)* basis in exchange for payment of $ *(storage fee)* per *(day, week, month, year)* payable on the first day of each such period.

3. The storage shall commence on *(first day of storage)* and shall continue until Owner claims Property or Bailee serves on Owner a ________ day written notice terminating this storage agreement. If Owner fails to claim Property on or before the last day of storage indicated in the notice, Bailee may (choose one):

   ☐ continue to store the property at the rate of $_______ per *(day, week, month or year)* until Property is claimed.

   ☐ deem Property to be abandoned, sell it to pay for outstanding storage fees and hold the balance for Owner.

4. If Owner claims Property during a period for which payment has been made, no prorata refund shall be made.

5. Bailee shall not deliver Property to any person other than Owner without prior written permission from Owner.

6. Property shall be stored at the following location: ______________________________

   Property shall not be removed from this location without prior written notice to and written consent of Owner. Property shall be stored under physical conditions which are designed to preserve it from damage, injury or theft.

7. Owner and Bailee agree that the approximate (check one)[35] ☐ replacement value ☐ fair market value each item of Property on the date this agreement is signed is: $ *(specify the value of each item described under Clause #1)* .

8. Property being stored appears to be in good condition except for the following defects or damage: *(describe any major defects)* .

9. In consideration for the compensation paid by Owner, Bailee shall (a) be fully responsible for returning Property to Owner in the same condition as it was when the storage commenced;[36] and (b) obtain insurance to protect Property against all commonly insurable losses, except *(put any specific type of loss which will not be insured, such as from floods or earthquakes)* .

10. The title to Property shall remain at all times in Owner.

11. If any dispute arises under the terms of this agreement, the parties agree to select a mutually agreeable neutral third party to help them mediate it.[37] If the mediation is deemed unsuccessful, the parties agree that (choose one):

    ☐ the dispute shall be decided by the applicable small claims court (or its equivalent)[38] if the amount in dispute is within the court's jurisdiction, and otherwise by binding arbitration under the rules issued by the American Arbitration Association. The decision of the arbitrator shall be final.

    ☐ the dispute shall be directly submitted to binding arbitration under the rules issued by the American Arbitration Association. The decision of the arbitrator shall be final.[39]

    ☐ the dispute shall be settled according to the laws of the state that apply to this agreement.[40]

    Any costs and fees (other than attorney fees) associated with mediation and arbitration shall be shared equally by the parties.

12. Attorney fees associated with arbitration or litigation shall be paid as follows (choose one):[41]

    ☐ Each party shall pay his or her own attorney fees.

    ☐ The reasonable attorney fees of the prevailing party shall be paid by the other party.

---

[35]See footnote 5, Sample Form 2.

[36]Unlike other bailment agreements in this chapter, this clause makes the bailee strictly liable for the condition of the property. This means that even if the property is accidently damaged or lost (for example, an errant communications satellite crashes through the garage roof and pulverizes it) the bailee must bear the cost. It is expected that the charge for this type of bailment will be higher than would otherwise be the case.

[37]See footnote 8, Sample Form 2.

[38]See footnote 9, Sample Form 2.

[39]See footnote 10, Sample Form 2.

[40]See footnote 11, Sample Form 2.

[41]See footnote 12, Sample Form 2.

13. All agreements between the parties related to storage of Property are incorporated in this contract. Any modification to this contract shall be in writing.[42]

14. Any provision in this contract found to be invalid shall have no effect on the validity of the remaining provisions.[43]

15. Additional terms for the storage of Property under this contract are as follows: *(describe additional terms not covered by other provisions)*.

Date	Date
Signature	Signature
Address	Address

[42] See footnote 13, Sample Form 2.

[43] See footnote 14, Sample Form 2.

FORM 6 **CONTRACT FOR BOARDING OF ANIMALS**

This contract is intended for use when someone needs to board his animal or animals with a friend, relative or neighbor for a significant length of time.

As with other contracts, the main purpose of this one is to get each party's expectations and obligations down on paper to forestall the possibility of a misunderstanding later. A sample agreement follows. A tear-out version is located at the end of the chapter.

SAMPLE FORM 6

ANIMAL BOARDING CONTRACT

1. *(Animal owner)*, Owner, desires to temporarily place the animal(s) designated in Clause 2 with *(person with whom pet is boarded)*, Bailee, from *(first day of boarding)* to (check one):

   ☐ *(last day of boarding)*.

   ☐ indefinitely.

2. The animal(s) subject to this agreement [Animal(s)] are: *(describe animal or animals)* .

3. Bailee agrees to care for Animal(s) for the time specified in Clause 1 in exchange for the following consideration (choose one or more):

   a. ☐ payment of $ *(flat amount, amount per week or month, etc.)* .

   b. ☐ reimbursement for reasonable out-of-pocket expenses, including veterinary bills, incurred while Animal(s) are being cared for.

   c. ☐ other valuable consideration in the form of: *(reciprocal acts, promises to perform an act, etc.)*.

4. Bailee shall provide Animal(s) with adequate food, shelter, exercise and veterinary care, as well as: ______________ .

5. If Owner claims Animal(s) during the period for which payment has been made under Clause 3, the payment will be refunded for the period of time after which the Animal(s) are returned to Owner.[44]

---

[44] For example, if the contract is terminated on ten days' notice a day after a month's payment has been made, the user will be entitled to a refund for the remaining 20-day period, or two-thirds of her monthly payment.

6. If Owner is unavailable to receive Animal(s) on the last day of boarding, Bailee may (choose one or more):

   ☐ continue to care for Animal(s) at a daily rate computed on the basis of the amount specified in Clause 3;

   ☐ turn the animal(s) over to *(name(s) of alternate persons or facilities)*

   and notify Owner in writing of the name and address of the person or facility to whom Animal(s) have/has been transferred.

   ☐ Serve Owner with a ________________ day notice of intent to sell Animal(s) and, if Animal(s) are not claimed by Owner within the notice period, sell Animal(s), apply the proceeds first to outstanding boarding costs and hold the balance for Owner.

7. Owner and Bailee agree that the approximate value of Animal(s) is $________________.

8. Animal(s) is/are in good physical condition except for the following:[45] *(describe illness or defect)*.

9. Bailee shall exercise reasonable care to protect Animal(s) from sickness, injury and theft. Responsibility for harm to Animal(s) that doesn't result from Bailee's breach of duty described in this clause shall be borne by Owner.

10. If any dispute arises under the terms of this agreement, the parties agree to select a mutually agreeable neutral third party to help them mediate it.[46] If the mediation is deemed unsuccessful, the parties agree that (choose one):

    ☐ the dispute shall be decided by the applicable small claims court (or its equivalents)[47] if the amount in dispute is within the court's jurisdiction, and otherwise by binding arbitration under the rules issued by the American Arbitration Association. The decision of the arbitrator shall be final.

    ☐ the dispute shall be directly submitted to binding arbitration under the rules issued by the American Arbitration Association. The decision of the arbitrator shall be final.[48]

    ☐ the dispute shall be settled according to the laws of the state that apply to this agreement.[49]

    Any costs and fees (other than attorney fees) associated with mediation and arbitration shall be shared equally by the parties.

---

[45]When an animal owned by one person is placed in the hands of another, it is very important for the parties to agree on the animal's condition. Months or years down the road the owner of the animal will tend to remember it as being in excellent physical condition whereas the possessor will remember its obvious and plentiful problems. The point of this clause is to prevent such painful misunderstandings.

[46]See footnote 8, Sample Form 2.

[47]See footnote 9, Sample Form 2.

[48]See footnote 10, Sample Form 2.

[49]See footnote 11, Sample Form 2.

11. Attorney fees associated with arbitration or litigation shall be paid as follows (choose one):[50]

    ☐ Each party shall pay his or her own attorney fees.

    ☐ The reasonable attorney fees of the prevailing party shall be paid by the other party.

12. All agreements between the parties related to boarding of Animal(s) are incorporated in this contract. Any modification to this contract shall be in writing.[51]

13. Any provision in this contract found to be invalid shall have no affect on the validity of the remaining provisions.[52]

14. Additional terms for the boarding of Animal(s) under this contract are as follows: *(describe additional terms not covered by other provisions or any special conditions, like check-ups, grooming, grazing requirements and insurance coverage)*.

Date	Date
Signature	Signature
Address	Address

[50]See footnote 12, Sample Form 2.

[51]See footnote 13, Sample Form 2.

[52]See footnote 14, Sample Form 2.

STORAGE CONTRACT

1. ______________________________, Owner, desires to store the following property (Property): ______________________________

____

____

2. ______________________________, Bailee, agrees to accept and store Property for Owner.

3. Property shall be stored at the following location: ______________________________

______________________________.

4. Bailee shall return Property to Owner at any time that either party desires.

5. The parties recognize that Bailee is not being directly compensated for his or her services. Bailee shall not be held liable to Owner for any damage to or theft of Property, no matter what the cause.

6. Any provision in this contract found to be invalid shall have no effect on the validity of the remaining provisions.

7. Additional terms for the storage of Property under this contract are as follows: ______________________________

____

____

______________________________ Date	______________________________ Date
______________________________ Signature	______________________________ Signature
______________________________ Address	______________________________ Address
______________________________	______________________________
______________________________	______________________________

STORAGE CONTRACT

1. ______________________________, Owner, desires to store the following property (Property):
____
____.

2. ______________________________, Bailee, agrees to store this property on a ______________ basis in exchange for payment of $ __________ per __________, payable on the first day of each such period.

3. The storage shall commence on ______________ and shall continue until Owner claims the property or Bailee serves a written __________ day notice terminating this storage agreement. If Owner claims the property in the middle of a period for which payment has been made, no prorata refund shall be made.

4. Property shall be stored at the following location: ______________________________
____.

5. Owner and Bailee agree that the approximate (check one) ☐ replacement value ☐ fair market value of each item of Property on the date this agreement is signed: $ ______________________________

6. Property being stored appears to be in good condition except for the following defects or damage: ______________
____
____.

7. Bailee shall exercise reasonable care to protect Property from theft or damage. Responsibility for theft and damage to Property that doesn't result from the Bailee's negligence shall be borne by Owner.

8. If any dispute arises under the terms of this agreement, the parties agree to select a mutually agreeable neutral third party to help them mediate it. If the mediation is deemed unsuccessful, the parties agree that (choose one):

   ☐ the dispute shall be decided by the applicable small claims court (or its equivalent) if the amount in dispute is within the court's jurisdiction, and otherwise by binding arbitration under the rules issued by the American Arbitration Association. The decision of the arbitrator shall be final.

   ☐ the dispute shall be directly submitted to binding arbitration under the rules issued by the American Arbitration Association. The decision of the arbitrator shall be final.

   ☐ the dispute shall be settled according to the laws of the state that apply to this agreement.

   Any costs and fees (other than attorney fees) associated with mediation and arbitration shall be shared equally by the parties.

9. Attorney fees associated with arbitration or litigation shall be paid as follows [choose one]:

- ☐ Each party shall pay his or her own attorneys' fees.
- ☐ The reasonable attorney fees of the prevailing party shall be paid by the other party.

10. All agreements between the parties related to the storage of Property are incorporated in this contract. Any modification to this contract shall be in writing.

11. Any provision in this contract found to be invalid shall have no affect on the validity of the remaining provisions.

12. Additional terms for the storage of Property under this contract are as follows: ______________________________

____

____.

______________________	______________________
Date	Date
______________________	______________________
Signature	Signature
______________________	______________________
Address	Address
______________________	______________________
______________________	______________________

STORAGE CONTRACT

1. ______________________________, Owner, desires to store the following property (Property):

____

____.

2. ______________________________, Bailee, agrees to store Property for payment by Owner of $ ______________. Payment shall be made on or before ______________________.

3. The storage shall commence on ______________ and continue until ______________, or until Owner claims Property, whichever occurs first.

4. If Owner fails to claim Property on or before the last day of storage indicated in Clause 3, Bailee shall continue to store Property at the rate of $ __________ per ____________ until Property is claimed or Bailee provides Owner with a ________ day written notice that the storage is being terminated and that Property will be sold if not claimed prior to the date specified in the notice.

5. If Owner fails to claim Property before the period specified in Clause 4 expires, Property shall be deemed abandoned. Bailee shall then sell Property, apply the proceeds to outstanding storage fees, and hold the balance for Owner.

6. If Property is claimed by Owner during any period for which payment has already been made, no prorata refund shall be made.

7. Property shall be stored at the following location: ______________________________

____.

Property shall not be removed from this location without prior written notice to and written consent of Owner.

8. Owner and Bailee agree that the approximate (check one) ☐ replacement value ☐ fair market value of each item of Property on the date this agreement is signed: $ ______________________________.

9. Property being stored appears to be in good condition except for the following defects or damage: ______________

____

____.

10. Bailee shall exercise reasonable care to protect Property from theft or damage. Responsibility for theft and damage to Property that doesn't result from Bailee's negligence shall be borne by the Owner.

11. If any dispute arises under the terms of this agreement, the parties agree to select a mutually agreeable neutral third party to help them mediate it. If the mediation is deemed unsuccessful, the parties agree that (choose one):

☐ the dispute shall be decided by the applicable small claims court (or its equivalent) if the amount in dispute is within the court's jurisdiction, and otherwise by binding arbitration under the rules issued by the American Arbitration Association. The decision of the arbitrator shall be final.

☐ the dispute shall be directly submitted to binding arbitration under the rules issued by the American Arbitration Association. The decision of the arbitrator shall be final.

☐ the dispute shall be settled according to the laws of the state that apply to this agreement.

Any costs and fees (other than attorney fees) associated with mediation and arbitration shall be shared equally by the parties.

12. Attorney fees associated with arbitration or litigation shall be paid as follows (choose one):

☐ Each party shall pay his or her own attorney fees.

☐ The reasonable attorney fees of the prevailing party shall be paid by the other party.

13. All agreements between the parties related to storage of Property are incorporated in this contract. Any modification of the contract shall be in writing.

14. Any provision in this contract found to be invalid shall have no affect on the validity of the remaining provisions.

15. Additional terms for the storage of Property under this contract are as follows: ______________________________

____

____.

______________________	______________________
Date	Date
______________________	______________________
Signature	Signature
______________________	______________________
Address	Address
______________________	______________________
______________________	______________________

STORAGE CONTRACT

1. ______________________________, Owner, desires to store the following property (Property):
____
____.

2. ______________________________, Bailee, agrees to store Property on a ______________ basis in exchange for payment of $ __________ per ______________ payable on the first day of each such period.

3. The storage shall commence on ______________ and shall continue until Owner claims Property or Bailee serves a __________ day written notice on Owner terminating this storage agreement. If Owner fails to claim Property on or before the last day of storage indicated in this notice, Bailee may (choose one):
   ☐ continue to store Property at the rate of $ __________ per ______________ until Property is claimed.
   ☐ deem Property to be abandoned, sell it to pay for outstanding storage fees, and hold the balance for Owner.

4. If Owner claims Property during the period for which payment has been made, no prorata refund shall be made.

5. Bailee shall not deliver Property to any person other than Owner without prior written permission from the Owner.

6. Property shall be stored at the following location: ______________________________
____.

   Property shall be stored under physical conditions which are designed to preserve it from damage, injury or theft.

7. Owner and Bailee agree that the approximate (check one) ☐ replacement value ☐ fair market value of each item of Property on the date this agreement is signed: $ ______________________________

8. Property appears to be in good condition except for the following defects or damage: ______________
____
____.

9. Bailee shall exercise reasonable care to protect the property from theft or damage. Responsibility for theft and damage to Property that doesn't result from Bailee's negligence shall be borne by Owner.

10. The title to Property shall remain at all times in Owner.

11. If any dispute arises under the terms of this agreement, the parties agree to select a mutually agreeable neutral third party to help them mediate it. If the mediation is deemed unsuccessful, the parties agree that (choose one):

☐ the dispute shall be decided by the applicable small claims court (or its equivalent) if the amount in dispute is within the court's jurisdiction, and otherwise by binding arbitration under the rules issued by the American Arbitration Association. The decision of the arbitrator shall be final.

☐ the dispute shall be directly submitted to binding arbitration under the rules issued by the American Arbitration Association. The decision of the arbitrator shall be final.

☐ the dispute shall be settled according to the laws of the state that apply to this agreement.

Any costs and fees (other than attorney fees) associated with mediation and arbitration shall be shared equally by the parties.

12. Attorney fees associated with arbitration or litigation shall be paid as follows (choose one):

☐ Each party shall pay his or her own attorney fees.

☐ The reasonable attorney fees of the prevailing party shall be paid by the other party.

13. All agreements between the parties relating to the storage of Property are incorporated in this contract. Any modifications to this contract shall be made in writing.

14. Any provision in this contract found to be invalid shall have no effect on the validity of the remaining provisions.

15. Additional terms for the storage of Property under this contract are as follows: ______________________________

____

____.

______________________	______________________
Date	Date
______________________	______________________
Signature	Signature
______________________	______________________
Address	Address
______________________	______________________
______________________	______________________

STORAGE CONTRACT

1. ______________________________, Owner, desires to store the following property (Property):________
____
____.

2. ______________________________, Bailee, agrees to store Property on a ____________________
basis in exchange for payment of $ ____________ per ______________ payable on the first day of each such period.

3. The storage shall commence on ____________________ and shall continue until Owner claims Property or Bailee serves on Owner a ______________ day written notice terminating this storage agreement. If Owner fails to claim Property on or before the last day of storage indicated in the notice, Bailee may
(choose one)
☐ continue to store the property at the rate of $ ______________ per ______________ until Property is claimed.
☐ deem Property to be abandoned, sell it to pay for outstanding storage fees, and hold the balance for Owner.

4. If Owner claims Property during a period for which payment has been made, no prorata refund shall be made.

5. Bailee shall not deliver Property to any person other than Owner without prior written permission from Owner.

6. Property shall be stored at the following location: ______________________________________
____.
Property shall not be removed from this location without prior written notice to and written consent of Owner. Property shall be stored under physical conditions which are designed to preserve it from damage, injury or theft.

7. Owner and Bailee agree that the approximate (check one) ☐ replacement value ☐ fair market value of each item of Property on the date this agreement is signed: $ ______________________________________

8. Property being stored appears to be in good condition except for the following defects or damage: ____________
____
____.

9. In consideration for the compensation paid by Owner, Bailee shall (a) be fully responsible for returning Property to Owner in the same condition as it was when the storage commenced; and (b) obtain insurance to protect Property against all commonly insurable losses, except ____
____.

10. The title to Property shall remain at all times in Owner.

11. If any dispute arises under the terms of this agreement, the parties agree to select a mutually agreeable neutral third party to help them mediate it. If the mediation is deemed unsuccessful, the parties agree that (choose one):

    ☐ the dispute shall be decided by the applicable small claims court (or its equivalent) if the amount in dispute is within the court's jurisdiction, and otherwise by binding arbitration under the rules issued by the American Arbitration Association. The decision of the arbitrator shall be final.

    ☐ the dispute shall be directly submitted to binding arbitration under the rules issued by the American Arbitration Association. The decision of the arbitrator shall be final.

    ☐ the dispute shall be settled according to the laws of the state that apply to this agreement.

    Any costs and fees (other than attorney fees) associated with mediation and arbitration shall be shared equally by the parties.

12. Attorney fees associated with arbitration or litigation shall be paid as follows (choose one):

    ☐ Each party shall pay his or her own attorney fees.

    ☐ The reasonable attorney fees of the prevailing party shall be paid by the other party.

13. All agreements between the parties related to storage of Property are incorporated in this contract. Any modification to this contract shall be in writing.

14. Any provision in this contract found to be invalid shall have no effect on the validity of the remaining provisions.

15. Additional terms for the storage of Property under this contract are as follows: ______________________________

    ____

    ____.

______________________	______________________
Date	Date
______________________	______________________
Signature	Signature
______________________	______________________
Address	Address
______________________	______________________
______________________	______________________

Animal Boarding Contract

1. ______________________________, Owner, desires to temporarily place the animal(s) designated in Clause 2 with ______________________________, Bailee, from ______________________________ to (check one)

   ☐ ______________________________.

   ☐ indefinitely.

2. The animal(s) subject to this agreement [Animal(s)] is/are: ______________________________
   ____
   ______________________________.

3. Bailee agrees to care for Animal(s) for the time specified in Clause 1 in exchange for the following consideration (choose one or more):

   ☐ a. payment of $ ______________.

   ☐ b. reimbursement for reasonable out-of-pocket expenses, including veterinary bills, incurred while Animal(s) is/are being cared for.

   ☐ c. other valuable consideration in the form of: ______________________________
   ______________________________.

4. Bailee shall provide Animal(s) with adequate food, shelter, exercise, and veterinary care, as well as: ______________________________
   ______________________________.

5. If Owner claims Animal(s) during the period for which payment has been made under Clause 3, the payment will be refunded for the period of time after which the Animal(s) are returned to Owner.

6. If Owner is unavailable to receive Animal(s) on the last day of boarding, Bailee may (choose one or more):

   ☐ continue to care for Animal(s) at a daily rate computed on the basis of the amount specified in Clause 3.

   ☐ turn the animal(s) over to ______________________________ and notify Owner in writing of the name and address of the person or facility to whom Animal(s) have/has been transferred.

   ☐ Serve Owner with a ______________ day notice of intent to sell Animal(s) and, if Animal(s) is/are not claimed by Owner within the notice period, sell Animal(s), apply the proceeds first to outstanding boarding costs, and hold the balance for Owner.

7. Owner and Bailee agree that the approximate value of Animal(s) is $ ______________.

8. Animal(s) is/are in good physical condition except for the following: ______________________________
   ____
   ______________________________.

9. Bailee shall exercise reasonable care to protect Animal(s) from sickness, injury and theft. Responsibility for harm to Animal(s) that doesn't result from Bailee's breach of duty described in this clause shall be borne by Owner.

10. If any dispute arises under the terms of this agreement, the parties agree to select a mutually agreeable neutral third party to help them mediate it. If the mediation is deemed unsuccessful, the parties agree that (choose one):

    ☐ the dispute shall be decided by the applicable small claims court (or its equivalents) if the amount in dispute is within the court's jurisdiction, and otherwise by binding arbitration under the rules issued by the American Arbitration Association. The decision of the arbitrator shall be final.

    ☐ the dispute shall be directly submitted to binding arbitration under the rules issued by the American Arbitration Association. The decision of the arbitrator shall be final.

    ☐ the dispute shall be settled according to the laws of the state that apply to this agreement;

    Any costs and fees (other than attorney fees) associated with mediation and arbitration shall be shared equally by the parties.

11. Attorney fees associated with arbitration or litigation shall be paid as follows (choose one):

    ☐ Each party shall pay his or her own attorney fees.

    ☐ The reasonable attorney fees of the prevailing party shall be paid by the other party.

12. All agreements between the parties related to boarding of Animal(s) are incorporated in this contract. Any modification to this contract shall be in writing.

13. Any provision in this contract found to be invalid shall have no affect on the validity of the remaining provisions.

14. Additional terms for the boarding of Animal(s) under this contract are as follows: ______________________________

    ____

    ____.

______________________	______________________
Date	Date
______________________	______________________
Signature	Signature
______________________	______________________
Address	Address
______________________	______________________
______________________	______________________

Chapter 5

Releases

his chapter provides release forms for use in the settlement of disputes.

A. What is a Release?

A common means of settling minor disputes (anything from an argument about an unpaid loan to a minor fender bender to a golf ball crashing through a plate glass window) is for one disputant to pay the other a sum of money to agree to give up his legal claim. For instance, if the paint on Tony's car is damaged when his neighbor Kate spray paints her fence, Tony might agree to release Kate from liability (that is, not sue Kate) if Kate agrees to pay $800 to have the car repainted. Or, if neighbors Tom and Carol jointly invest $1,000 in a rototiller and Tom hogs and then breaks the machine, Carol might agree not to take Tom to small claims court if Tom repays her share.

Of course, disputes don't have to be settled by one person agreeing to pay the other money. It is not uncommon to settle a minor claim by having one person do something for the other. To return to the example of the rototiller, Tom and Carol might settle their dispute by Tom agreeing both to fix the rototiller and help Carol get her garden in.

WARNING! The releases in this chapter are not appropriate to release claims based on events that haven't occurred yet. For instance, if you enroll in a skydiving school, you will probably be required to sign a release stating that the school has no liability for any injuries you may suffer. This kind of release must often be individually drafted with considerable care and even then may not be fully enforceable.

B. Releases Contained in This Chapter

This chapter contains the following releases:

FORM 1: General Release. For settling most types of disputes where one person has a claim against another.

FORM 2: General Mutual Release. For disputes when each party has a claim against the other.

FORM 3: Release for Damage to Real Estate. For settling claims for damages to a person's house or land caused by a neighbor's activity.

FORM 4: Release for Property Damage in Auto Accident. For settling fender benders when no one has been injured.

FORM 5: Mutual Release of Contract Claims. For settling disputes that arise under a contract.

FORM 6: Release for Minor Personal Injuries. For settling minor injury claims arising from auto accidents, dog bites, etc.

In this chapter, we provide a sample of each of these types of releases, along with a brief discussion and suggested language to complete them. Tear-out versions of each release are located at the end of this chapter.

C. When Releases Are Enforceable

Because releases are contracts, they are only binding if courts are willing to enforce them. This commonly depends upon several variables. Let's briefly consider them.

Voluntariness. A fundamental principle of contract law is that each side must enter into the agreement voluntarily. If a party has been pressured into signing an agreement because of the superior bargaining position of the other or for some other reason, a court may consider it involuntary. For example, insurance adjusters have been known to wave a big pile of small bills under the nose of financially needy and poorly educated accident victims to pressure them into signing releases, knowing the victim would surely recover much more if they filed a lawsuit. When challenged in court, such releases are sometimes held to be unenforceable.

Fairness. In addition, certain basic rights are often deemed too important to contract away. This is especially true when the party signing a release doesn't fully appreciate the extent of his injury or damage or the magnitude of the rights he is waiving. For instance, if a person suffers a serious concussion in an automobile accident and two days later signs a release tendered by the insurance company in exchange for a settlement of $500, few courts will bind the victim to this agreement. A good general way to think about whether a particular release will be enforced is to ask yourself if, broadly speaking, the settlement is fair to both parties. If it isn't, you may have an enforceability problem.

Type of Claim. As a general rule, no release based on a personal injury should ever be signed until a doctor has examined the injured person, clearly established the scope of the injury and stated that the person has fully recovered. For instance, if a person suffers a bump on the head, the examination report should state that no more extensive harm is likely (that is, no brain damage or hemorrhage has occurred and enough time has passed to be sure there will be no long-term problem). It is particularly unwise from the legal point of view (and even illegal in some states) to obtain a release soon after an accident from an injured person without a doctor's opinion.

The situations for which the releases in this book are intended should not give rise to voluntariness or fairness problems. However, if you have any reason to suspect that a release you wish to have signed might be considered to be unfair and therefore unenforceable, check it out with an attorney first.

D. Look Before You Leap

By now you've probably gathered that releases are powerful documents. Suppose that in exchange for $500 you release your neighbor from liability for damage caused by erosion of your property caused by runoff from his land. Then, six months later, you discover that the foundation to your house is in jeopardy from this same runoff. Can you sue your neighbor for the $50,000 worth of repairs necessitated by the runoff? No, you can't, unless the release is declared unenforceable for one of the reasons discussed above.

Of course, in most situations the stakes are not so high, and a release can be comfortably signed with the knowledge that the dispute will be finally laid to rest. However, it is always wise to ask the following questions before you sign on the dotted line:

- Do you fully understand what the release accomplishes?
- Do you fully understand the potential extent of the harm you have suffered?
- Do you understand what the law provides in such situations if you choose to go to court rather than settle?
- Have you discussed your decision to sign the release with someone with good business sense or, if a lot of money or important legal rights are involved, with an attorney?
- If you reworded one of our form releases, have you checked the result with a lawyer?

If the answer to any of these questions is a "no," or even a waffling "maybe," we urge you to do the necessary homework before releasing the other party from liability.

E. Provisions In Our Leases

All releases in this chapter contain the primary elements discussed below. Most of them contain one or more additional clauses specific to that type of release. Here is a brief discussion of the clauses and language common to all our releases:

1. The names and addresses of the party being released and the party granting the release.
2. A brief description of the "what," "when" and "where" of the dispute or issue to which the release pertains.

   Each release provides several blank lines for you to briefly describe the events giving rise to the need for the release. See the sample form releases below.
3. A statement of what the person giving up a claim is getting in return.

   For a release to be a valid contract (which it must be to be enforceable) the person signing the release (releasor) must receive something of benefit (called "consideration" by lawyers) in exchange for her agreement to give up her right to sue. Each of our releases provides a space for this "consideration" to be described. Typically, it is money. If so, simply enter the amount. If it is an agreement by the releasee to perform or not perform some act (for example, stop his dog from barking at night), describe the act. Examples of suggested language are provided with samples of the forms provided below.
4. A statement that the release applies to all claims arising from the dispute or issue, both those known at the time the release is signed and those that may come along later. This provision is very common in releases; without it they wouldn't be worth much.
5. A statement that the release binds all persons who might otherwise have a legal right to file a claim on behalf of the releasor (for example, the releasor's spouse or heirs).

   Our forms use the following language to make this statement:

   "In executing this release I intend to bind my spouse, heirs, legal representatives, assigns, and anyone else claiming under me, in addition to myself."

Although we have included this provision in each of our releases for caution's sake, it is rare that it will ever prove relevant. In fact, such persons are usually bound by the release anyway. It's important to remember, however, that listing these people in a release does not affect any rights that such persons may otherwise have in their own behalf. Thus, in community property states, both spouses should sign every release. See Section F, below.

ASSIGNMENT NOTE: A person's "assigns" are those to whom he has legally given (assigned) specified rights. A person's right to sue (termed a "cause of action") often may be assigned to others, especially if it arises under a contract. If the right to sue has been assigned to another party before the release is signed, the other party is not bound by the release. On the other hand, if the release is signed first and the assignment is made later, the assignment means nothing, because the assignor has already given up (released) his right to sue—he has nothing to assign. To protect the releasee, each release contains a statement that no assignment of the releasor's claims has been made.

6. A statement applying the benefits of the release to all persons who are legally entitled to share them with the person being released (for example, the releasee's heirs).

   This statement is made in the following language:

   "I also intend that this release apply to the heirs, personal representatives, assigns, insurers or successors of the releasee named below, as well as to the releasee."

   As with the previous section, this language is included for completeness even though it is rarely relevant. It makes clear that the scope of the release extends to people whose rights might be asserted on behalf of the releasee.

7. The date the release is signed.
8. The signature and addresses of the parties.

   It is not required for both parties to sign a release when only one of them is granting it. However, we think it important that both parties sign off on this important document since there are statements in it which jointly apply to them. However, if the person being released does not want to sign, the release will still be valid, except for the mutual releases (Forms 2 and 5) where the signatures of both parties are definitely required.

WARNING! By now we hopefully have impressed upon you how important it is that the context in which a release is signed be fair. If a release involves a lot of money or a potentially large claim, you may want to bolster the chances of its being upheld (should it ever be challenged later), by signing it in front of a witness or two who can later testify, if the issue arises, that the other party was under no duress and appeared to know what he was doing. If your release involves a small claim, it is not necessary to do this. To encourage you to have your release witnessed where appropriate, we have included two lines on each release for witnesses to sign. If you decide to dispense with witnesses, put "N.A." on each of the lines.

F. Obtaining Signature of Spouse in Community Property States

In community property states (states which treat most property owned by married couples as community property) a claim for damage to community property can not be fully released unless both husband and wife sign the document. Each of our releases, while speaking in the singular, provides a place for a spouse to sign. Thus, if you are the releasor and live in California, Idaho, New Mexico, Texas, Arizona,

Nevada, Washington, Louisiana or Wisconsin, make sure your spouse signs the release as well as yourself.

NOTE: Before you proceed to the forms, carefully read Chapter 1 for instructions on how to fill them in.

FORM 1 GENERAL RELEASE

This form is appropriate for settling personal disputes over a contract, debt or minor personal injury when only one party is alleged to have been injured or suffered damage. Here is a sample with some suggestions for how to fill it out.

SAMPLE FORM 1

GENERAL RELEASE

1. *(Person signing release)*, Releasor, voluntarily and knowingly execute this release with the express intention of eliminating Releasee's liabilities and obligations as described below.

2. Releasor hereby releases *(person being released)*, Releasee, from all claims, known or unknown that have arisen or may arise from the following occurrence: *(description of events giving rise to release, including location and date if appropriate)*

Sample Language:

a. "Repair work incompletely done to Releasor's boat at the Fixemup shipyards on 5/6/87."

b. "Agreement by Releasee made during the week of June 6, 19— to deliver the fully laid out and pasted-up manuscript for the book Do Your Own Brain Surgery to Releasor's address no later than July 6, 19—, which Releasee failed to keep."

c. "A tree growing on Releasee's property at 1011 Oak St. fell into Releasor's backyard at 1013 Oak St. on August 7, 19—. It damaged Releasor's fence, which had to be replaced. The tree itself had to be removed by ABC Tree Terminators."

3. In exchange for granting this release Releasor has received the following consideration: *(amount of money, or description of something else of value which person signing release received from other party)*

> *Sample Language:*
>
> *a.* "$150 cash".
>
> *b.* "a used Philco television set."
>
> *c.* "an agreement by (Releasee's name) to desist from further activities as described in Clause 3 of this release."
>
> *d.* "an agreement by (Releasee's name) to repair Releasor's Apple IIe computer by January, 19—."

4. In executing this release Releasor additionally intends to bind his or her spouse, heirs, legal representatives, assigns and anyone else claiming under him or her. Releasor has not assigned any claim covered by this release to any other party. Releasor also intends that this release apply to the heirs, personal representatives, assigns, insurers and successors of Releasee as well as to the Releasee.

This release was executed on ____________________, 19____ at *(city and state)*.

____
Releasor's Signature

____
Address

____

____

____
Releasee's Signature

____
Address

____

____

____
Releasor's Spouse's Signature

Witnesses:

____
Name

____
Address

____
Name

____
Address

FORM 2 GENERAL MUTUAL RELEASE

This form is appropriate for settling disputes over a contract, debt or minor personal injury where each party claims that the other is at fault and that each suffered damage or injury as a result. For instance, if John spends ten hours fixing Allen's car, and Allen thinks the car runs worse than it did before and refuses to pay John, the interests of both Allen and John have suffered. A sample of FORM 2 follows. A tear-out version is located at the end of this chapter.

SAMPLE FORM 2

GENERAL MUTUAL RELEASE

1. We, ____

and ____,

voluntarily and knowingly execute this mutual release with the express intention of eliminating the liabilities and obligations described below.

2. Disputes and differences that we mutually desire to settle have arisen between us with respect to the following: *(description of the event and problem giving rise to the release)*

____

____

> *Sample Language:*
>
> *a.* "responsibility for damages to three valuable artworks owned by (person's name) and stored with ____________ under a long-term storage agreement signed by (person's name) on January 23, 19— and by (person's name) on January 25, 19—.
>
> *b.* "damages resulting from an automobile accident on February 1, 19— at the intersection of Grove and Alma streets in Anytown, Ohio, in which cars owned by the parties were involved."
>
> *c.* "repairs undertaken by (person's name) during the week of March 15, 19— on the engine of a 19— Toyota Tercel owned by (person's name), which the owner considers to be unsatisfactory."

3. The consideration for this mutual release is as follows:

   a. Mutual relinquishment of our respective legal rights with reference to the disputes and differences described above; and

   b. Other valuable consideration.[1]

4. In exchange for this consideration, each of us expressly releases the other, and his/her heirs, insurers and legal representatives from all claims known or unknown to us that have arisen or may arise from the transaction described in Clause 2. In executing this release we intend to bind our spouses, heirs, legal representatives, assigns and anyone else claiming under us, in addition to ourselves. Neither of us has assigned a claim arising from the transaction described in Clause 2 to another party.

5. We have executed this release on ____________________, 19____ at *(city and state)*.

---

[1]n mutual releases, it is not necessary to put out the specific consideration received by the parties since each party benefits from the release granted by the other.

Releasor's Signature	Releasee's Signature
Address	Address
Releasor's Spouse's Signature	

Witnesses:

Name	Address
Name	Address

FORM 3 RELEASE FOR DAMAGE TO REAL ESTATE

This form is appropriate for settling disputes between landowners that arise when one owner's property is damaged by another owner's action or inaction (for example, an overhanging tree, an improper diversion of water, or commercial activity), or when the dispute is over whose responsibility it is to fix a common wall or fence.[2] A sample of FORM 3 follows. A tear-out version is located at the end of this chapter.

[2]For a detailed discussion of rights and obligations enjoyed by neighbors, see *Neighbor Law* by Cora Jordan, Nolo Press.

SAMPLE FORM 3

RELEASE FOR DAMAGE TO REAL ESTATE

1. *(Person doing the releasing)*, Releasor, voluntarily and knowingly executes this release with the express intention of eliminating Releasee's liabilities and obligations as described below.

2. Releasor hereby releases *(person being released)*, Releasee, from all claims, known or unknown to Releasor that have arisen or may arise from the transaction described in Clause 4.

3. Releasor is the owner of certain property (Property) located at *(street, city, county, state)* ________, which specifically consists of *(a brief description of the real estate)*.

> *Sample Language:*
>
> *a.* "a residential lot 60 feet wide and 120 feet deep with a house"
>
> *b.* "an unimproved rural plot of approximately 5 acres"
>
> *c.* "a 40' stationary mobile home manufactured by Chieftan"

4. Releasor has alleged that Property suffered damage in the approximate amount of $________ as a result of the following activity of Releasee: *(brief description of alleged activity)*

> *Sample Language:*
>
> *a.* "Releasee failed to keep the portion of the storm drain on his property clear of debris, which clogged the drain and caused flooding on Releasor's property."
>
> *b.* "Releasee failed to properly maintain a large eucalyptus tree in his backyard with the result that a large branch broke off and damaged the roof on Releasor's house."
>
> *c.* "Releasee has not paid her share of fixing a fence common to backyards belonging to Releasee and Releasor which Releasor believes to be in need of repair."

5. In executing this release Releasor additionally binds his or her spouse, heirs, legal representatives, assigns and anyone else claiming under him or her. Releasor has not assigned any claim arising from the transaction described in Clause 4 to another party. In addition to Releasee, this release extends to Releasee's heirs, successors, insurers and personal representatives.

6. Releasor has received good and adequate consideration for this release in the form of: *(money, services, agreement for future conduct, etc.)*

____

This release was executed on ____________________, 19____ at ____*(city and state)*____.

______________________	______________________
Releasor's Signature	Releasee's Signature
______________________	______________________
Address	Address
______________________	______________________
______________________	______________________

____
Releasor's Spouse's Signature

Witnesses:

______________________	______________________
Name	Address
______________________	______________________
Name	Address

FORM 4 RELEASE FOR PROPERTY DAMAGE IN AUTO ACCIDENT

This form should be used when you wish to settle claims over minor property damage from an auto accident. For instance, suppose Hank's car bumps into Betty's car in a parking lot and puts a dent in Betty's door. Betty obtains an estimate of $200 to fix the dent. If Hank pays Betty the $200, he should have Betty sign this release stating that payment is in full settlement of all claims. This form should not be used when personal injuries are involved (See Section C above). In the case of minor personal injuries, use FORM 6. A sample of FORM 4 follows. A tear-out version is located at the end of this chapter.

SAMPLE FORM 4

RELEASE FOR PROPERTY DAMAGE IN AUTO ACCIDENT

1. *(Name of person making the release)*, Releasor, voluntarily and knowingly executes this release with the express intention of eliminating the Releasee's liabilities and obligations as described below.

2. Releasor hereby releases *(name of person being released)*, Releasee, from all liability for claims, known and unknown, arising from property damage sustained by Releasor in an automobile accident that occurred on *(date of accident)* at *(location of accident)* ______________ involving a vehicle owned by Releasee, or driven by Releasee or his/her agent.

3. This release applies only to property damage and does not apply to any claim for personal injuries, physical or emotional, which Releasor had, has, or may have as a result of the accident described in Clause 2.

4. By executing this release Releasor does not give up any claim that he or she may now or hereafter have against any person, firm or corporation other than Releasee and those persons and entities specified in Clause 7.[3]

5. Releasor understands that Releasee does not, by providing the consideration described below, admit any liability or responsibility for the accident described in Clause 2 or its consequences.[4]

---

[3]Other people or companies in addition to the other driver are often liable for damage to your car. For instance, if the other driver's brakes had just been repaired but failed, the mechanic, as well as the other driver, might be liable. This statement makes clear that your release only applies to the person named (and those legally associated with her).

[4]This statement allows the other driver to settle with you for your property damage without admitting any blame in the event you have personal injuries and later decide to sue.

6. Releasor has received good and adequate consideration for this release in the form of *(describe form of consideration, such as money, goods or services)* ________

____

> *Sample Language:*
>
> *a.* "$500 cash."
>
> *b.* "a used Panasonic 26" television set."
>
> *c.* "an agreement by the *(name of person)* to repair Releasor's Apple IIe computer by January, 19—."

7. In executing this release Releasor additionally intends to bind his or her spouse, heirs, legal representatives, assigns and anyone else claiming under him or her. Releasor has not assigned any claim arising from the accident described in Clause 2 to any other party. This release applies to Releasee's heirs, legal representatives, insurers and successors, as well as to Releasee.

8. This release was executed on ________________, 19____ at *(city and state)*.

Releasor's Signature	Releasee's Signature
Address	Address
________________	________________
________________	________________
Releasor's Spouse's Signature	

Witnesses:

Name	Address
Name	Address

FORM 5 MUTUAL RELEASE OF CONTRACT CLAIMS

This form can be used to settle a disagreement that arises from a written or oral contract. For instance, if John and Frank agree that John will paint signs on ten of Frank's trucks for a specified sum per truck, and Frank backs out of the deal after the fifth truck, John and Frank could use this release to help solve their differences. Unlike the general release (FORM 1) or the general mutual release (FORM 2), this release is specific to contract disputes. A filled-out sample of this form follows. A tear-out version is located at the end of this chapter.

SAMPLE FORM 5

MUTUAL RELEASE OF CONTRACT CLAIMS

1. We, *(either party's name)* and *(other party's name)*, voluntarily and knowingly execute this mutual release with the express intention of eliminating the liabilities and obligations described below.

2. Disputes and differences have arisen between us with respect to the *(oral or written)* agreement entered into between the parties on *(date agreement was made or signed)*, under which the parties agreed to the following: *(briefly describe nature of the contract)*.

   This agreement is hereby made a part of this release and incorporated by reference. A copy of the agreement (if written) is attached to this release.

3. Each party hereby expressly releases the other from all claims and demands, known and unknown, arising out of the agreement specified in Clause 2.

4. This release additionally applies to our heirs, legal representatives and successors and is binding on our spouses, heirs, legal representatives, assigns and anyone else claiming under us. Neither of us has assigned to another party any claim arising under or out of the contract specified in Clause 2.

5. The consideration for this mutual release is a) our mutual agreement to forgo our respective legal rights with reference to the disputes and differences described above, and b) other valuable consideration.[5]

6. We also agree that the contract specified in Clause 2 shall be and is hereby rescinded, terminated, and cancelled as of *(date contract is no longer to be in effect)*[6]

7. We have executed this release on ____________, 19___ at *(city and state)* ____________.

---

[5]In mutual releases, it is not necessary to put out the specific consideration received by the parties since each party benefits from the release granted by the other.

[6]This statement makes clear that the contract under which the dispute arose is no longer in effect, by mutual agreement. The date of termination can be retroactive if the parties desire.

Releasor's Signature

Address

Releasee's Signature

Address

Releasor's Spouse's Signature

Witnesses:

Name

Address

Name

Address

FORM 6 RELEASE FOR PERSONAL INJURY

This release may be used when one party has suffered a relatively minor personal injury because of another's actions. In Section C, we stressed that releases involving personal injuries should only be signed when the parties are sure that the scope of the injury is fully known. Should a "minor" injury in fact later turn out to be a major one, the person who prematurely signed the release will be very sorry. In some instances, a release signed in these circumstances can be set aside in court, but this by no means always happens. Nonetheless, for injuries that are clearly limited in scope (for example, a minor dog bite that has completely healed if a doctor agrees that there will be no further problem), this release is appropriate.

CAUTION: Some attorneys are very good at making minor injuries into major ones. If the injured person is concerned about getting the greatest possible recovery under the circumstances, he should consult an attorney who specializes in personal injury cases.

SAMPLE FORM 6

RELEASE FOR PERSONAL INJURY

1. *(Name of person making the release)*, Releasor, voluntarily and knowingly executes this release with the express intention of eliminating the Releasee's liabilities and obligations as described below.

2. Releasor hereby releases *(name of person being released)*, Releasee, from all liability for claims, known and unknown, arising from injuries, mental and physical, sustained by Releasor as described below: *(describe injury and events that caused it)*

Sample language:

a. "A German Shepherd dog belonging to Releasee bit Releasor's left arm, puncturing the skin, when Releasor attempted to stop the dog from entering his house."

b. "Releasor's car collided with Releasee's car at the intersection of 5th and Vine, causing Releasor to bruise his sternum when he struck the steering wheel."

c. "Releasee's newspaper printed certain untrue information about Releasor which caused Releasor emotional distress."

3. Releasor has been examined by a licensed physician or other health care professional competent to diagnose (choose one or more):

☐ physical injuries and disabilities

☐ mental and emotional injuries and disabilities.

Releasor has been informed by this physician or health care professional that the injury described in Clause 2 has mended without causing permanent damage.

4. By executing this release Releasor does not give up any claim that he/she may now or hereafter have against any person, firm or corporation other than Releasee.[7]

---

[7] Other people or companies may also be liable for injuries. For instance, if the injury results from a car accident, and the other driver's brakes had just been repaired but failed, the mechanic, as well as the other driver, might be liable. This statement makes clear that your release only applies to the person named.

5. Releasor understands that Releasee does not, by providing the consideration described below, admit any liability or responsibility for the above described injury or its consequences.[8]

6. Releasor has received good and adequate consideration for this release in the form of *(describe form of consideration, such as money, goods or services)*

> *Sample Language:*
>
> *a.* "$500 cash."
>
> *b.* "a used Panasonic 26" television set."
>
> *c.* "an agreement by the *(name of person)* to repair Releasor's Apple IIe computer by January, 19—."

7. In executing this release Releasor additionally intends to bind his/her spouse, heirs, legal representatives, assigns and anyone else claiming under him/her. Releasor has not assigned any claim arising from the events described in Clause 2 to any other party. This release applies to Releasee's heirs, legal representatives, insurers, assigns and successors as well to Releasee.

8. This release was executed on ____________________, 19___ at *(city and state)* ________________________.

Releasor's Signature	Releasee's Signature
Address	Address

Releasor's Spouse's Signature

Witnesses:

Name	Address
Name	Address

[8]This statement allows the releasee to settle without admitting blame. This is important since the releasee may not wish to make such an admission in light of her employment, insurance rates, or in the event the Releasor changes his mind and decides to try and break the release.

GENERAL RELEASE

1. ______________________________, Releasor, voluntarily and knowingly execute this release with the express intention of eliminating Releasee's liabilities and obligations as described below.

2. Releasor hereby releases ______________________________, Releasee, from all claims, known or unknown that have arisen or may arise from the following occurrence: ______________________________
____
______________________________.

3. In exchange for granting this release Releasor has received the following consideration: ______________________________
____
______________________________.

4. In executing this release Releasor additionally intends to bind his or her spouse, heirs, legal representatives, assigns, and anyone else claiming under him or her. Releasor has not assigned any claim covered by this release to any other party. Releasor also intends that this release apply to the heirs, personal representatives, assigns, insurers and successors of Releasee as well as to the Releasee.

5. This release was executed on ______________________, 19______ at ______________________
______________________________.

______________________	______________________
Releasor's Signature	Releasee's Signature
______________________	______________________
Address	Address
______________________	______________________
______________________	______________________

____
Releasor's Spouse's Signature

Witnesses:

______________________	______________________
Name	Address
______________________	______________________
Name	Address

GENERAL MUTUAL RELEASE

1. We, ____

   and ____,

   voluntarily and knowingly execute this mutual release with the express intention of eliminating the liabilities and obligations described below.

2. Disputes and differences that we mutually desire to settle have arisen between us with respect to the following: ____________

   ____

   ____

   ____.

3. The consideration for this mutual release is as follows:

   a. Mutual relinquishment of our respective legal rights with reference to the disputes and differences described above; and

   b. Other valuable consideration.

4. In exchange for this consideration, each of us expressly releases the other, and his/her heirs, insurers and legal representatives from all claims known or unknown to us that have arisen or may arise from the transaction described in Clause 2. In executing this release we intend to bind our spouses, heirs, legal representatives, assigns, and anyone else claiming under us, in addition to ourselves. Neither of us has assigned a claim arising from the transaction described in Clause 2 to another party.

5. We have executed this release on ____________________, 19______ at ____________

   ____.

______________________________	______________________________
Releasor's Signature	Releasee's Signature
Address	Address
______________________________	______________________________
______________________________	______________________________

____
Releasor's Spouse's Signature

Witnesses:

______________________________	______________________________
Name	Address
Name	Address

RELEASE FOR DAMAGE TO REAL ESTATE

1. ______________________________, Releasor, voluntarily and knowingly execute this release with the express intention of eliminating Releasee's liabilities and obligations as described below.

2. Releasor hereby releases ______________________________, Releasee, from all claims, known or unknown to Releasor that have arisen or may arise from the transaction described in Clause 4.

3. Releasor is the owner of certain property (Property) located at ______________________________ ______________________________, which specifically consists of ______________________________ ______________________________.

4. Releasor has alleged that Property suffered damage in the approximate amount of $ __________ as a result of the following activity of Releasee: ______________________________ ______________________________ ______________________________.

5. In executing this release Releasor additionally binds his or her spouse, heirs, legal representatives, assigns, and anyone else claiming under him or her. Releasor has not assigned any claim arising from the transaction described in Clause 4 to another party. In addition to Releasee, this release extends to Releasee's heirs, successors, insurers and personal representatives.

6. Releasor has received good and adequate consideration for this release in the form of: ______________________________ ______________________________ ______________________________.

7. This release was executed on ______________________________, 19 _______ at ______________________________ ______________________________.

____
Releasor's Signature

____
Address

____

____

____
Releasee's Signature

____
Address

____

____

____
Releasor's Spouse's Signature

Witnesses:

____
Name

____
Address

____
Name

____
Address

RELEASE FOR PROPERTY DAMAGE IN AUTO ACCIDENT

1. ______________________________, Releasor, voluntarily and knowingly execute this release with the express intention of eliminating Releasee's liabilities and obligations as described below.

2. Releasor hereby releases ______________________________, Releasee, from all liability for claims, known and unknown, arising from property damage sustained by Releasor in an automobile accident that occurred on ______________ at ______________________________ ______________________ involving a vehicle owned by Releasee, or driven by Releasee or his/her agent.

3. This release applies only to property damage and does not apply to any claim for personal injuries, physical or emotional, which Releasor had, has, or may have as a result of the accident described in Clause 2.

4. By executing this release Releasor does not give up any claim that he or she may now or hereafter have against any person, firm or corporation other than Releasee and those persons and entities specified in Clause 7.

5. Releasor understands that Releasee does not, by providing the consideration described below, admit any liability or responsibility for the accident described in Clause 2 or its consequences.

6. Releasor has received good and adequate consideration for this release in the form of ______________________ ____ ____.

7. In executing this release Releasor additionally intends to bind his or her spouse, heirs, legal representatives, assigns, and anyone else claiming under him or her. Releasor has not assigned any claim arising from the accident described in Clause 2 to any other party. This release applies to Releasee's heirs, legal representatives, insurers and successors, as well as to Releasee.

8. This release was executed on ______________________, 19______ at ______________________ ____.

____
Releasor's Signature

____
Address

____

____

____
Releasee's Signature

____
Address

____

____

____
Releasor's Spouse's Signature

Witnesses:

____
Name

____
Address

____
Name

____
Address

MUTUAL RELEASE OF CONTRACT CLAIMS

1. We ____ and ____ voluntarily and knowingly execute this mutual release with the express intention of eliminating the liabilities and obligations described below.

2. Disputes and differences have arisen between us with respect to the ____________________ agreement entered into between the parties on ____________________, under which the parties agreed to the following: ____________________ ____.

   This agreement is hereby made a part of this release and incorporated by reference. A copy of the agreement (if written) is attached to this release.

3. Each party hereby expressly releases the other from all claims and demands, known and unknown, arising out of the agreement specified in Clause 2.

4. This release additionally applies to our heirs, legal representatives, and successors and is binding on our spouses, heirs, legal representatives, assigns, and anyone else claiming under us. Neither of us has assigned to another party any claim arising under or out of the contract specified in Clause 2.

5. The consideration for this mutual release is a) our mutual agreement to forgo our respective legal rights with reference to the disputes and differences described above, and b) other valuable consideration.

6. We also agree that the contract specified in Clause 2 shall be and is hereby rescinded, terminated, and cancelled as of ______________________________.

7. We have executed this release on ____________________, 19______ at ____________________ ____.

______________________________	______________________________
Releasor's Signature	Releasee's Signature
______________________________	______________________________
Address	Address
______________________________	______________________________
______________________________	______________________________

____
Releasor's Spouse's Signature

Witnesses:

______________________________	______________________________
Name	Address
______________________________	______________________________
Name	Address

RELEASE FOR PERSONAL INJURY

1. ______________________________, Releasor, voluntarily and knowingly executes this release with the express intention of eliminating the Releasee's liabilities and obligations as described below.

2. Releasor hereby releases ______________________________, Releasee, from all liability for claims, known and unknown, arising from injuries, mental and physical, sustained by Releasor as described below:

____

______________________________.

3. Releasor has been examined by a licensed physician or other health care professional competent to diagnose (choose one or more):

   ☐ physical injuries and disabilities

   ☐ mental and emotional injuries and disabilities.

   Releasor has been informed by this physician or health care professional that the injury described in Clause 2 has mended without causing permanent damage.

4. By executing this release Releasor does not give up any claim that he/she may now or hereafter have against any person, firm or corporation other than Releasee.

5. Releasor understands that Releasee does not, by providing the consideration described below, admit any liability or responsibility for the above described injury or its consequences.

6. Releasor has received good and adequate consideration for this release in the form of ______________________________

____

______________________________.

7. In executing this release Releasor additionally intends to bind his/her spouse, heirs, legal representatives, assigns, and anyone else claiming under him/her. Releasor has not assigned any claim arising from the events described in Clause 2 to any other party. This release applies to Releasee's heirs, legal representatives, insurers, assigns and successors as well to Releasee.

8. This release was executed on ____________________, 19______ at ______________________________

______________________________.

Releasor's Signature

Releasee's Signature

Address

Address

Releasor's Spouse's Signature

Witnesses:

Name

Address

Name

Address

Chapter 6

Contracts For Home Repairs, Maintenance and Remodeling

This chapter includes four agreements that cover home maintenance, repairs, remodeling and other work you want done at your residence such as painting or gardening.

The truth is, major misunderstandings between a homeowner and contractor can arise at every turn if the main issues haven't been worked out in advance. Most people have heard stories about the kitchen remodeling job that took twice as long and cost twice as much as originally anticipated, and the roof that was promised before the rainy season and completed in the spring.

But the more specific you are about the details of the job in advance, the more assured you are of getting the work done right, on time and within your budget. This chapter helps you do all that, whether you use our contract forms to negotiate an oral understanding or actually get the agreement in writing, as we strongly recommend.

CHOOSING A CONTRACTOR. This chapter does not help you choose the best contractor for your job. However, the National Association of Home Builders (15th and M Streets, NW, Washington DC 20005; (202) 822-0200) publishes a free brochure, *How to Choose a Remodeler Who's on the Level,* which will help you select a home improvement contractor. If your state agency licenses or registers home improvement and repair work, it may provide information on complaints filed against individual contractors or publish a consumer's guide that will help you arrange for home repair work. Finally, contact your local Better Business Bureau for the track record of contractors you're considering hiring.

A. Contracts in this Chapter

Here is a brief description of each contract contained in this chapter:

1. Contract for Home Maintenance.

Use for jobs lasting a day or two, such as hauling refuse, cleaning a garage or house, washing windows, gardening and other work. Such jobs are usually performed by one person.

2. Contract for Simple Home Repairs.

Use for jobs lasting two to three days which involve little or no materials, including minor electrical wiring, non-structural carpentry repairs, touch-up painting, masonry work, and roofing repairs. Such jobs are usually performed by one person.

3. Contract for Moderate Home Repairs.

Use for skilled jobs lasting one to two weeks which involve considerable materials, including landscaping, and the installation of irrigation systems, decks and balconies, as well as for interior alterations such as a new doorway or knocking down a wall. Such jobs are usually performed by one person but sometimes require a specialized subcontractor—such as a plumber for an irrigation system.

4. Contract for Extensive Home Repairs or Remodeling.

Use for skilled jobs lasting two weeks or more which involve major work such as additions, kitchen remodeling, a new roof, and complete exterior or interior painting. Such jobs almost always require a general contractor and a number of subcontractors—such as electricians, plumbers and masons.

The term "contractor" is used in this chapter to describe the person who will be responsible for getting the work done, even though the person may not be a licensed contractor or general contractor.

B. How to Use the Contracts in this Chapter

The forms in this chapter can be used in several different ways.

1. **As a checklist for analyzing any contract that is proposed by a contractor.** Large firms, especially those doing major home repairs and remodeling, will usually want you to use their own contracts. If you insist on using our form instead of theirs, some contractors won't work with you. But it is certainly appropriate to discuss how the contracts differ and to add or delete clauses from the contractor's form. The information in this chapter will help you do that intelligently. And if a contractor insists on a strict take-it-or-leave-it approach that clashes with your own plans, look elsewhere.
2. **As the actual contract.** If the contractor doesn't offer a contract, or is agreeable to using another contract, consider using one of the forms in this chapter. They are easy to fill in using the instructions given here—and can be clearly understood by everyone involved.

3. **As a general checklist of important items.** The contractor may not wish to work under a written contract, perhaps because of an aversion to such formality, or maybe because he or she doesn't feel up to figuring out what the contract means. If you decide to proceed with a contractor under an oral agreement, the forms in this chapter will help you clarify important terms before work begins.

The more money and time involved in the job, the more you need a written contract. Although oral agreements are common for simple jobs such as rubbish hauling, spot carpentry, touch up painting and a day's worth of gardening (covered by Contracts 1 and 2), they are definitely not advised for more long-term work involving skilled labor and expensive materials (covered by Contracts 3 and 4).

Although oral contracts for home maintenance, repair and remodeling are almost always legally enforceable, both the homeowner and contractor may have difficulty remembering the details of their agreement. If they end up in arbitration or court it is likely to be one person's word against the other. And if the arbitrator, judge or jury can't determine what was originally intended, the specific terms of the agreement—whatever it was—won't be enforced. So, if possible, get it in writing.

INFORMAL LETTERS: If the idea of a written contract is all that is standing between you and a contractor, try this approach. Make an oral agreement based on the form in this chapter that is most appropriate for the work being done. Take notes. Then, write the contractor an informal letter, repeating your understanding of the agreement. Ask the contractor to let you know if there's anything wrong or missing. Although the letter is not the equivalent of a formal contract, it can be used as a starting point for discussion if a dispute later arises, and can also be used as evidence of your agreement if the matter ends up in arbitration or in court.

C. Legal Status of Workers

The contracts in this chapter assume that the person responsible for doing the work is an independent contractor rather than your employee. The difference between these two categories is difficult to describe in the abstract. It depends heavily on rules of, and decisions by, the Internal Revenue Service, as well as on the laws of each individual state that affect unemployment insurance and workers' compensation benefits. But the difference is important.

For big jobs, there may be two levels of responsibility—for the person you contract with to get the job done, and for the workers that person uses for specialized portions of the job. For instance, you may contract with a contractor to add a wing to your home. That contractor, in turn, will arrange for plumbers and electricians to install the pipes and wiring. These specialized workers are termed subcontractors, and the contracts in this book assume that they also are independent contractors or employees of the contractor rather than your employees.

Employers have a number of legal obligations to employees, which may include paying for workers' compensation insurance, contributing to state and federal benefit programs such as unemployment and Social Security, maintaining health and safety standards and withholding federal and state income taxes. None of these obligations are owed to independent contractors, who are considered self-employed. One who hires an independent contractor must, however, fill out and file an IRS Form 1099 for every contractor who is paid $600 or more in a calendar year. The contractor is responsible for declaring and paying taxes on his or her income.

When called on to decide whether a person is an employee or an independent contractor, federal and state agencies examine up to 20 different factors. As a general rule, a contractor will be considered an independent contractor rather than your employee if he or she:

- operates a business at a definite location—as evidenced by such things as a business name, stationery, cards, signs, and advertising
- owns the tools, supplies and equipment required for the job and
- works free from your direct supervision, being responsible only for the quality of the final result you are paying for.

Also as a general rule, someone you hire to do a one-time job lasting a day or two will qualify as an independent contractor. But even a single repetitive task, such as weeding a garden twice a month, may lead to the classification of the worker as an employee and thus trigger the requirements that appropriate benefits be provided. Needless to say, the rule that casual laborers are to be treated as employees is commonly more honored in its breach than its observance, but of course you can't count on this.

Of more practical importance, most states have threshold amounts of hours worked and wages paid—for example, 60 hours a quarter—which trigger a worker's classification as an employee. You can quickly check the rule by calling your state's Department of Employment or Department of Labor Standards. If there is such a threshold, be careful not to exceed it in your agreement, assuming that the worker is more likely an employee than an independent contractor. For example, if you contract with a teenager to paint your house under your supervision, you would limit the work to 60 hours a month or whatever your state's threshold is to avoid having your new worker legally classified as an employee.

See Chapter 7, Sections B and C for a more detailed discussion of when someone is an employee under state and federal laws, employers' legal obligations to employees and the potential consequences of treating an employee as an independent contractor.

D. Regulation of Home Contractors

State oversight of home repair firms and contractors can vary widely, from no or minimal involvement to skills-based licensing or certification. While a heavy regulatory apparatus doesn't guarantee that a home repair job will be done competently, it usually does provide the homeowner with some recourse if the job is done wrong. If there is no regulation at all, however, the homeowner may be left to live with—and pay for—the botched job.

This section provides information about:

- what home repair regulation normally consists of
- the states in which some form of regulation exists and
- what protections regulation provides for consumers.

If you want more specific information about how your state regulates home repair and remodeling contractors, find out the name of your state's regulatory agency (for instance, State Contractors Licensing Board) and contact it for more information. Your State Consumer Protection Office (see the list in the Appendix) should steer you to the appropriate agency. If there is a state agency regulating home repair and remodeling contractors, it will usually have free consumer pamphlets available for the asking.

1. How States Regulate Home Repairs

Some states require people who do home repair and remodeling work to register with the state. Registration usually does not require any demonstration of experience or training. It is primarily designed to keep track of people offering contractor services so that homeowners can locate them if something goes wrong during or after the job is done.

A number of other states go beyond regulation and require a license to do specified types of work.

Almost all states have licensing requirements for certain categories of home improvement and repair work. For example, most states license people who do residential electrical and plumbing work. On the other hand, only about a third of the states have licensing requirements for contractors who do general repair and remodeling work, such as framing, dryboard installation, panelling, deck construction, siding and painting.

Among the states that require a license for general repair and remodeling tasks, requirements for the license vary. But most require some experience and skills training, and some evidence of financial responsibility or effective customer recourse policy.

STATES WITH SOME TYPE OF REGISTRATION OR LICENSING REQUIREMENT FOR GENERAL HOME REPAIR AND REMODELING WORK

(For details, contact your state agency that oversees contractors)

Alabama	Hawaii	North Dakota
Alaska	Iowa	Oregon
Arizona	Maryland	Rhode Island
Arkansas	Michigan	South Carolina
California	Nebraska	Tennessee
Connecticut	Nevada	Utah
Delaware	New Jersey	Virginia
District of Columbia	New Mexico	Washington
Florida	North Carolina	

MORE LOCAL CONTROLS: In some states, local ordinances may impose registration or licensing requirements on some types of contractors. For information on local ordinances, contact your local building or planning department.

License and registration requirements are often tied to:

- Size of the job—for example, a license may be required for work on any job over $5,000.
- Type of job. Some states require a license for commercial work but not for residential work.
- Type of customer recourse—for instance, the state may require the contractor to carry general liability insurance or contribute to a customer recovery fund as a condition of keeping a license.
- Location of contractor. Most states regulate contracting work of any type that is done by out-of-state contractors.

2. Advantages of Using a Licensed or Registered Contractor

From the homeowner's standpoint, it is often a good idea to use licensed or registered contractors in the states that have these requirements. (In California, those who are selling their houses must disclose to prospective buyers all work done by unlicensed contractors.)

First, a license may signal that the contractor has had to demonstrate some skills or experience. Also, licensed and registered contractors must normally offer their customers—as a condition of obtaining the license or registration—some type of recourse for inadequate or shoddy work.

Each state that licenses or registers contractors—except Alabama, Connecticut, Iowa and Michigan—requires its contractors to provide some or all of the following customer protections:

- Insurance for damage or injury to customer or customer's property.
- A performance bond—that is, a guarantee backed by a third party (usually an insurance company) that the contractor will do the job right. The guarantee is usually limited to between $1,000 and $5,000.
- A showing of financial solvency that enables the company to pay any judgments related to the work.

Also, in these states, if there is a problem with the contractor's performance, you can urge the state licensing or registration board to mediate the dispute or even take some disciplinary action against the contractor—although this is rare. If you use an unlicensed contractor, on the other hand, there is no one to complain to.

There is, of course, one major advantage to using unlicensed contractors: They usually cost a lot less than the licensed variety, perhaps as little as half the price.

A few of the states that require a license also require the contractors to inform their customers about various rights, obligations and pitfalls of dealing with a contractor. (See Section F.)

3. Liability for On-the-Job Injuries

Who is responsible if the contractor is injured while performing the job? There is no simple answer to this question. It primarily depends on:

- what and who caused the accident,
- what the contract says about allocation of this responsibility, and
- what status (employee or independent contractor) the contractor is found to have. As a general rule, independent contractors are supposed to carry their own insurance, and most home repair contracts provide that the homeowner not be held responsible for injuries to the contractor. But if a contractor is injured and applies for workers' compensation insurance, you may be held liable if it is established that the contractor was legally your employee rather than a true independent contractor.

The simple truth about injuries suffered during home construction is that the law generally sees to it that someone other than the injured person pays the medical bills and possibly much more. Fortunately, the typical homeowner's or renter's insurance policy provides coverage for injuries suffered by people performing casual home repairs. For more extensive repairs, however, the renter's or homeowner's policy may not apply. You should double-check your own policy by calling your insurance agent before you enter into a contract. And, as we point out in Section H, you definitely should require proof that contractors and subcontractors doing work under Contracts 3 and 4 have their own workers' compensation and general liability insurance.

E. Mechanic's and Materials Liens

A mechanic's lien is a claim that is recorded at the county land records office against a home by someone who has done work on it. A materials lien is a claim that is recorded by someone who has supplied materials for the work. Unfortunately, both types of liens occur fairly commonly during major construction or remodeling work on a home.

For instance, a contractor can record a lien against your home if you decide to withhold final payment—perhaps because the work is substandard, or unfinished, or not what you agreed to have done. Once a lien is placed on your home, your "title" to the home is considered "encumbered," and you may have trouble borrowing against the home or selling it until you get the lien removed by paying the contractor.

It's important to understand that paying the contractor for all labor and materials doesn't protect you against the possibility of a lien if the contractor fails to pay subcontractors used on the job or suppliers of materials. These people too have the right to record a lien against your home if they aren't paid for their work or materials, regardless of whose fault the non-payment is. To get rid of the subcontractors' or materials suppliers' liens, you might have to pay them separately, even though you already paid the contractor for the work or supplies.

Example: Paul hires Mazursky Contractors Inc. to remodel his kitchen. Halfway through the job, Paul becomes unhappy with the work and replaces Mazursky with another contractor. Mazursky bills Paul for work already done, and Paul refuses to pay on the ground that the work already performed was unsatisfactory. Mazursky, in turn, doesn't pay Eddie Electrician for work Eddie did, and Eddie doesn't pay Acme Electrical, his supplier for the electrical supplies used on the job. Mazursky, Eddie and Acme are all entitled to file liens against Paul's house until they get paid for their work and materials.

Clearly, liens are better left avoided. The best way to do this is to make sure that those associated with the home repair—contractors, subcontractors, materials providers—are paid and that your contract protects you against liens being recorded against your home.

Liens are mainly an issue with moderate or extensive home repairs and remodeling. Contracts 3 and 4 offer these alternative ways to deal with the liens issue:

a. The final payment to the contractor should be withheld until the contractor provides either (1) lien waivers (or releases) from the contractor and all subcontractors and materials providers or (2) acknowledgement from these people that they have been fully paid. In essence, this approach makes the contractor responsible for protecting you from liens.

b. All periodic payments to the contractor are conditioned upon the receipt of lien waiving (releases) from subcontractors and materials suppliers involved in the phase of the work being paid for.

c. All checks written to the contractor shall be jointly written in the names of the contractor, subcontractors and materials suppliers. This approach requires the contractor to pay the subcontractors and materials providers as a condition of getting paid herself, since all payees must endorse the check if any of them are to be paid.

d. The contractor should be prohibited from using any subcontractors without first obtaining a lien waiver, or purchasing any materials without first obtaining an "acknowledgement of full payment." The contractor shall show the homeowner copies of the waiver or acknowledgement before work is performed or materials used. This approach prevents work or materials from being provided without advance protection against liens.

These aren't the only options. You and the contractor may also agree to another approach to protect you against liens, such as having the contractor and all subcontractors sign an agreement that liens will only be imposed after the dispute resolution mechanisms provided for in the contract have been used.

In most cases, the first or second approach are the best. They place full responsibility on the contractor to protect you against liens as a condition of receiving payments due under the contract. The other approaches may be more difficult for you or the contractor to carry out. But in some situations, the contractor will prefer one of them to the first two. The point is, you want to protect yourself as much as possible against the possibility that the contractor will fail to pay the subcontractors and materials suppliers, leaving you holding the bag—with a lien on your home.

F. State and Local Requirements for Home Repairs and Remodeling

1. State Requirements

A few states either impose specific requirements on home repair and remodeling agreements, or at least require contractors to inform their customers of certain rights they have and the consequences of not paying for work done or supplies delivered.

For example, Hawaii requires contractors to inform their customers of:

- the contractor's right to place liens on the property
- whether the contractor is bonded and, if not, the extent of financial security available to assure performance of the contract
- the customer's right to demand that the contractor post a bond that will guarantee the quality of the contractor's work
- the approximate percentage of work to be subcontracted
- the contractor's license number and classification
- the exact dollar amount of the contract
- the date work is to begin and number of days for completion, and
- the scope of work to be performed and materials to be used.

Maryland, Washington, Oregon, California and a few other states also require some of these express notifications.

The contracts used in this chapter account for many of these issues, but they don't take the place of any specific notice to customers required by a state's laws. It's up to the contractor to know these specific requirements—and to obey them. Again, if you want to know more about your state's rules, contact your state agency that handles contractor licensing or registration.

2. Local Requirements—Permits and Approvals

As a general rule, a homeowner must obtain a permit from a city agency before major home repairs can begin. Also, if the house is part of a condominium complex or planned unit development, formal approval of the work by a homeowner's association or "architectural review committee" will also be necessary if the work affects the home's exterior appearance.

For instance, building permits are usually required for jobs that involve structural alterations, additions (a new room), substantial remodeling (a kitchen or bathroom), or new electrical wiring or plumbing installations. And homeowner association approval is usually necessary for new windows, exterior painting, roofing and additions.

Permits, however, are usually not required for casual carpentry, minor plumbing and electrical repairs, or adding a new window or door.

Either you or the contractor must be responsible for getting information about the necessary permits. It's imperative that you know whether permits are required and who is going to obtain them. The best place to inquire about permit requirements is your local planning or building department. If the job requires a permit or approval, but none is obtained, the homeowner may have to redo all or a portion of the work if a later inspection reveals deficiencies. Also, the value of the home may be adversely affected when it comes to resale if the buyer learns of the non-permit work.

G. What to Do if the Contract is Broken

If services are not fully performed as described in the contract, it is necessary to determine whether the flaw is large enough to justify refusing to pay the remaining contract balance. The law uses a concept called "substantial performance" to determine whether a party to a contract has basically fulfilled obligations.

If a court or arbitrator determines that there has been "substantial performance," it orders payment of the balance, minus the amount it determines to be equivalent to the work not performed. If, on the other hand, the court or arbitrator decides that substantial performance has not occurred, then no payment at all is ordered.

Generally, how these disputes come out depends on how trivial the incompleteness appears relative to the overall task. Unfortunately, it's impossible to give guidelines that will let you determine whether or not a contract has been substantially performed. No matter how specific your contract, there are bound to be some grey areas. On the other hand, much more often than not—those involved can usually agree on whether a job has been substantially performed.

Where this issue is relevant, the contracts in this chapter handle the problem of completion by:

- encouraging all involved to completely describe the services to be performed, and
- giving the person paying for the services the right to condition final payment upon personal satisfaction—but requiring good faith in making this determination. The more specific the description of services to be performed, the less discretion the person paying for the services will have to refuse payment.

Contracts 3 and 4 also let the parties decide how disputes about completion and other elements of the contract should be resolved. Language is provided for the following options:

1. Mediation

Mediation is a process in which two people with a dispute meet with a neutral third person in an effort to settle the dispute. The mediator has no power to impose a decision, only to try to help the parties arrive at one. If both sides agree, a settlement contract is drawn up and everyone, if not happy, is at least minimally satisfied. Professional mediation services can be found in the Yellow Pages, and courts are starting to offer experimental mediation services, although most of these are restricted to family law disputes.

2. Arbitration

Arbitration is like court, but it involves one or three arbitrators instead of a judge and is considerably cheaper and faster than the courts, although the arbitrators must be paid. Those involved in the dispute can select their own arbitrator or arbitrators, if there is someone they agree on, or apply to an organization that provides arbitrators—such as the American Arbitration Association. Normally, the arbitrator's decision is final.

3. Small Claims Court

Small claims court is the cheapest and easiest way to resolve minor disputes involving money—most courts will handle cases involving $2,000 or less, although some will hear disputes involving as much as $10,000. The procedures can be handled without an attorney, and many small claims courts bar attorneys from representing those involved.

4. Regular Court Proceedings

Every state has one or more courts in which breach of contract actions can be filed. More often than not, this process is long, expensive and seldom produces any winners—except perhaps the attorneys who are usually necessary to handle the case.

H. Indemnification

When extensive home repairs are made, there is always a question as to what happens if other people or their property are injured as a result. For instance, suppose the truck carrying lumber for your new kitchen crunches your neighbor's car while turning into your driveway. It is common for home repair contracts to allocate responsibility for injuries and damages to the independent contractor who has control over whether the performance is prudent and responsible. Your would shift responsibility by including an indemnification or "hold harmless" clause in your contract.

This arrangement does not affect the right of the other person—the neighbor whose car was damaged—to seek recovery from both you and the contractor. However, if you, as homeowner, are held liable, an indemnification provision allows you to obtain reimbursement from the contractor. As a kind of safety net, if the contractor does not carry insurance, your homeowner's insurance policy may cover your liability for injuries caused to others, but it's better not to rely on this.

The message from these general principles is clear. Liability for injuries to others, while always possible, can be best avoided by assuring yourself that the person really is an independent contractor, and making sure he or she carries insurance. When considering any extensive home repair or remodeling, it is wise to insist upon a Certificate of Insurance from your contractor. This Certificate should name you as an additional insured under the Contractor's Liability Policy.

Especially for work done under Contracts 3 and 4, it is also wise to require proof that the contractor and any subcontractors are covered by their own workers' compensation policies. As we mentioned in Section D, extensive work on the home may not be covered under your homeowner's insurance policy, leaving you personally liable for any injuries suffered by uncovered workers who are considered to have been employees rather than independent contractors.

I. Choosing Which Contract to Use

This section outlines the four types of contracts provided in this chapter. The contracts differ according to the complexity of the work to be performed. Although it is possible to use Contract 4—Contract for Extensive Home Repairs or Remodeling—for casual work, you will find yourself stumbling over lots of clauses that really aren't necessary. On the other hand, if you use Contract 1—Contract for Home Maintenance—for a new addition to your home, you will definitely have failed to address a number of serious issues that arise out of extensive remodeling work.

Contract 1: Home Maintenance

Contract 1 is intended for unskilled labor on a one-time job that isn't expected to last for more than one or two days and doesn't involve the need for materials.

Contract 2: Simple Home Repairs

Contract 2 covers home repairs done by skilled labor —carpenter, plumber, electrician, painter, mason— for a job that isn't expected to take more than a few days. If significant materials are required in addition to the labor, Contract 3 (Moderate Home Repairs) should be used, but if the materials are not especially important or a significant part of the cost, use Contract 2.

Contract 3: Moderate Home Repairs

Contract 3 is useful for skilled jobs that involve both labor and materials and that aren't expected to take more than a week or two to complete. Examples are landscape and irrigation systems, decks and minor but structural interior alterations. If the work doesn't involve much material, and isn't expected to last more than a few days, Contract 2 may be more appropriate. On the other extreme, if the work is expected to last more than a week or two, Contract 4 may be the more appropriate.

Contract 4: Extensive Home Repairs or Remodeling

Contract 4 is useful for skilled jobs that involve both labor and materials and that are expected to take more than two weeks to complete. Examples are additions to the home, a complete kitchen remodeling, major landscape jobs and a complete repainting. If the work is moderate but expected to last less than two weeks, Contract 3 may be the more appropriate.

J. Instructions for Completing the Contracts

The following are step-by-step instructions on how to fill out the contracts for home repairs, maintenance and remodeling.

Contract 1: Home Maintenance

Begin by providing details on the people involved and the location of the home maintenance work.

a. In the first blank, enter your own name. For the rest of the contract, you will be referred to as "Homeowner."

b. Enter the name of the person who has agreed to do the work—to be called "Contractor" for purposes of the contract.

c. Enter your street address. Include the city, state and zip code.

1. Job Description

To guard against future misunderstandings, your agreement should contain a specific description of the service or repair work. For work that is likely to last a day or less, the description should be straightforward. For example:

For gardening: "Cutting and edging the lawn, trimming the hedge on the north, east, and west sides of the property, weeding and conditioning the flower gardens (both front yard and back), trimming the fruit trees in the back yard, and all necessary watering."

For external cleaning and hauling: "Remove and haul all debris from back yard and garage, scrub and wash all external walls, remove ivy from fence on north boundary of property, sweep concrete surface in back yard, and sweep garage."

If you have a variety of odds and ends that don't fit in the space provided, attach a list of the jobs and enter this language in the contract: "See attached list of jobs."

2. Payment Terms

Unskilled laborers generally get paid in one of three ways:

a. at the end of the job

b. half at the beginning of the job and half at the end or

c. an hourly rate with maximum wages and payment schedule specified.

Check the appropriate box and then fill in the relevant information, including method of payment —cash or check.

3. Time of Performance

Specify the day and hour the work is to begin and the day and hour it is to end. This will usually be the same day.

4. *Independent Contractor Status*

In this clause you specify that the contractor is an independent contractor and check off the items that support this conclusion. Be sure to read Section C of this chapter for a more detailed discussion of the legal status of independent contractors. Although you can't make an employee into an independent contractor by completing this clause, you can use it to clarify your view of the contractor's legal status.

5. *Additional Agreements and Amendments*

This clause allows you to describe other agreements you and the contractor have reached. For example, you may want to provide that the contractor bring a certain tool to the job, or that you will pay actual costs of taking garbage to the city dump.

Also, you may wish to add information to one or more of the clauses already in the contract by first writing in: *Contractor and Homeowner add the following language to Clause ___.* Insert the language that describes your additional agreement, then add this sentence: *This additional language shall apply in case of a conflict between it and existing language in Clause ____.*

For example, if you want to specify that if the job isn't done on time as required in Clause 3, no further payment will be made, insert the following language here:

Contractor and Homeowner add the following language to Clause 3: If the time limits in this clause are not met by Contractor, Homeowner shall not be obligated to make any further payment for the work, regardless of how much has been done. This additional language shall apply in case of a conflict between it and existing language in Clause 2.

If you wish to add additional clauses to this contract, perhaps from one of the other contracts in this chapter, take the following steps:

- Label a blank 8 1/2" by 11" piece of paper "Attachment A".
- Reproduce on Attachment A the clause or clauses you wish to use in this contract, and fill them in.
- Use the following language in this clause to make Attachment A part of this contract: *Contractor and Homeowner incorporate the clauses set out on Attachment A as if fully set out herein.*
- Sign or initial (both you and the contractor) each clause on Attachment A.

Finally, the last clause provides that all agreements between you and the contractor have been made part of this written contract and that any changes in or additions to the contract must be in writing. These provisions prevent either you or the contractor from contradicting the plain terms of this contract by arguing that a separate oral agreement was made before the contract was signed, or that an oral amendment was made to the contract after it was signed.

Contract 2: Simple Home Repairs

Begin by providing details on the people involved and the location of the home repair work.

a. In the first blank, write in your own name. For the rest of the contract, you will be referred to as "Homeowner."

b. Write in the name of the person who has agreed to do the work—to be called "Contractor" for purposes of the contract.

c. Write in your street address. Include the city, state and zip code.

1. *Job Description*

The description should reflect the joint efforts of you and the contractor. Once you agree as to what you want and what the contractor will do for the price, put the result here. Here are some sample descriptions:

For electrical work: "Replace existing 110 volt outlets in living room, kitchen, and laundry room with 220 volt outlets; replace 110 volt ungrounded outlets in bedrooms with 110 volt grounded outlets, and run new line into downstairs office, using 60 gauge wire."

For carpentry: "Repair door frame and install new door so that there is no space around the door and so the door is firmly in place when shut. Replace window frames and sashes in the kitchen."

2. *Payment Terms*

Skilled labor generally gets paid in one of three ways:

- at the end of the job
- half at the beginning of the job and half at the end or
- an hourly rate with maximum wages and payment schedule specified.

Check the appropriate box and then fill in the relevant information, including method of payment—cash or check.

3. *Time of Performance*

Contracts for one-time simple home repairs should specify the day the work is to begin and the day it is to end, if more than one day. Specify these dates in the blanks provided. The clause also provides that "Time is of the essence," which means that you are serious about the times specified in the contract and reserve the right to sue for damages if the job isn't completed on time.

4. *Independent Contractor Status*

In this clause you specify that the contractor is an independent contractor and check off the items that support this conclusion. If you aren't able to check most of the items, the chances are excellent that the person is—legally—an employee rather than an independent contractor, unless the amount paid for the job falls below the statutory threshold. Be sure to read Section C of this chapter for a more detailed discussion of what constitutes an independent contractor. Although you can't make an employee into an independent contractor by completing this clause, you can use it to clarify your view of the contractor's legal status.

5. *License Status and Number*

If the work is being done by a plumber, electrician, or a person who advertises as a licensed contractor, it is a good idea to specify the license, by type and number. If a dispute arises as to the quality of the work, you may have some recourse with the state licensing board. See Section D above for a discussion of licensing requirements and potential recourse.

If there is no license requirement for the type of work being done, the third box should be checked and reasons provided.

If a license is required but the worker isn't licensed, simply don't use this clause. But see Section D for reasons why it is good to use licensed personnel when a license is required.

6. *Liability Waiver*

This clause states that the contractor is responsible for his or her own injuries. If a court or state agency later determines that you as the homeowner are responsible anyway, your homeowner's insurance policy may cover the loss. (See Section D.3 for a discussion of liability issues.)

7. *Permits and Approvals*

This clause lets you specify who will research local permit and approval requirements, who will obtain what permits and approvals necessary, and who will pay for them. Because the repairs covered by this contract are minor, it is more likely than not that no building permit will be required. If that is definitely the case, cross out the clause. (See Section F.2 for a discussion on permits and approvals.)

8. *Additional Agreements and Amendments*

This clause allows you to describe other agreements you and the contractor have reached. For instance, if you own a farm, you may want to be more specific about the hours that a saw or drill can be used, since that type of noise might interfere with a particular farm routine. Or if you are allergic to certain substances, you may want to specify that they not be used.

Also, you may wish to add information to one or more clauses already written in the contract. Do so by first writing in: *Contractor and Homeowner add the following language to Clause ___.* Insert the language that describes your additional agreement. Then add this sentence: *This additional language shall apply in case of a conflict between it and existing language in Clause ____.*

For example, if you want to specify that if the job isn't done on time as specified in Clause 3, no further payment will be made, insert the following language here:

Contractor and Homeowner add the following language to Clause 3: If the time limits in this clause are not met by Contractor, Homeowner shall not be obligated to make any further payment for the work, regardless of how much has been done. This additional language shall apply in case of a conflict between it and existing language in Clause 2.

If you wish to add additional clauses to this contract, perhaps from one of the other contracts in this chapter, take the following steps:

- Label a blank 8 1/2" by 11" piece of paper "Attachment A".
- Reproduce on Attachment A the clause or clauses you wish to use in this contract, and fill them in.
- Use the following language in this clause to make Attachment A part of this contract: *Contractor and Homeowner incorporate the clauses set out on Attachment A as if fully set out herein.*
- Sign or initial (both you and the contractor) each clause on Attachment A.

Finally, the last part of this clause provides that all agreements between you and the contractor have been made part of this written contract and that any changes in or additions to the contract must be in writing. These provisions prevent either you or the contractor from contradicting the plain terms of this contract by arguing that a separate oral agreement was made before the contract was signed, or that an oral amendment was made to the contract after it was signed.

Contract 3: Moderate Home Repairs

Begin by providing details on the people involved and the location of the home repair work.

a. In the first blank, write in your own name. For the rest of the contract, you will be referred to as "Homeowner."

b. Write in the name of the person who has agreed to do the work—to be called "Contractor" for purposes of the contract.

c. Write in your street address. Include the city, state and zip code.

1. Job Description

For moderate home repairs, a description of the work can be hard to come by. A starting place is the contractor's estimate. This typically will consist of a total amount for labor and materials and separate amounts for each component. It is often wise to ask the contractor to make a more detailed list of what she plans to do to accomplish the particular job. You'll also want to see illustrations or blueprints, depending on the job. This is specially important for projects involving considerable design, such as a fancy deck or landscaping.

After you review, understand and approve this list and design, it can easily be incorporated into this clause of the contract. Write the following:

The services to be performed under this contract are fully set out in Attachment 1 to this agreement, entitled "Project Design," which is incorporated in this contract by reference.

2. Payment Terms

Contractors who perform moderate home repairs not lasting longer than a week or two generally get paid in one of several ways:

a. A contract amount for the total job, payable at its satisfactory completion, including labor and materials.

> **Example**: *Contractor agrees to build a deck for Homeowner. The entire cost of the deck will be $5,000, including all labor and materials, payable upon satisfactory completion and approval by owner.*

b. A contract amount for total labor, payable at satisfactory completion of the job, plus materials as purchased.

> **Example**: *Contractor agrees to build a deck for Homeowner. The labor on the deck will be $2,000, payable upon completion. The materials for the deck will cost a maximum of $3,000, payable upon delivery to the worksite.*

c. A contract amount for the total job, including labor and materials payable in several installments—for example 25% at the beginning of the job and 25% when certain defined aspects of the job are completed, and 50% upon final completion.[1]

Example: *Contractor agrees to build a deck for Homeowner. The total job will cost $5,000, including labor and materials—payable $1,500 in advance, $1,500 when the support for the deck is completed, and $2,000 when the deck is satisfactorily completed and approved by the Homeowner.*

d. A contract amount for total labor, payable in installments, plus cost for materials as incurred.

Example: *Contractor agrees to build a deck for homeowner. The total labor for the deck shall cost $2,000, $500 payable in advance, $500 payable when the support for the deck is completed, and $1,000 upon satisfactory completion and approval by the homeowner. Materials shall be paid for by Homeowner at the time of delivery to the worksite.*

e. Time actually spent, billed at an hourly rate up to a specified maximum, plus cost of materials.

Example: *Contractor agrees to build a deck for homeowner. Contractor shall bill Homeowner for time spent, at the rate of $25 an hour, but no more than $2,000, and for materials at the time they are delivered to the worksite.*

Check the appropriate boxes and then fill in the relevant information, including method of payment—cash or check.

[1]If your state regulates home repair and remodeling contractors, it may limit the amount that can be charged as a down payment. Check with your state's regulatory agency.

NOTE: Although payment for materials is covered in Clause 2, Clause 9 describes the materials to be used.

3. *Time of Performance*

Contracts for moderate home repairs should specify the day the work is to begin and the day it is to end. Specify these dates in the spaces provided. The contract also states that "Time is of the essence," which means that you are serious about the times specified in the contract and reserve the right to sue for damages if the job isn't completed on time.

4. *Independent Contractor Status*

In this clause you specify that the contractor is an independent contractor and check off the items that support this conclusion. If you aren't able to check most of the items, the chances are excellent that the person is—legally—an employee rather than an independent contractor. Be sure to read Section C of this chapter for a more detailed discussion of what constitutes an independent contractor. Although you can't make an employee into an independent contractor by completing this clause, you can use it to clarify your view of the contractor's legal status.

5. *License Status and Number*

If the work is being done by a plumber, electrician, or a person who advertises as a licensed contractor, use this blank to describe the license by type and number. If a dispute arises as to the quality of the work, you may have some recourse with the state licensing board. See Section D above for a discussion of licensing requirements and potential recourse.

If there is no license requirement for the type of work being done, that box should be checked and reasons provided. If the contractor is not licensed, but the job calls for a license, skip over this clause.

6. *Liability Waiver*

This clause states that the contractor is responsible for his or her own injuries to the fullest extent possible under the law. (See Section D.3 for a discussion of who is liable for on-the-job injuries.)

NOTE: If the contractor is using subcontractors or employees, or the work risks injuries to neighbors or others, you may wish to also use the indemnification clause set out in Contract 4. That clause makes the contractor responsible for claims against you by other parties, and lets you require the contractor to obtain business liability insurance, listing you as a co-insured, and workers' compensation insurance if necessary.

To add the indemnification clause to this contract, follow the directions provided for Clause 13 (Additional Agreements and Amendments).

7. *Permits and Approvals*

This clause lets you specify who will research local permit and approval requirements, who will obtain what permits and approvals are necessary, and who will pay for them. Because the repairs covered by this contract are moderate, it is likely that a building permit will be required, at least for some part of the work. And if the work affects the home's exterior appearance and the home is part of a condominium complex or planned unit development, approval by an architectural review committee will probably be necessary. (See Section F.2, above)

If no permit or approval is necessary, simply skip over this clause.

8. *Liens and Waivers of Liens*

This contract offers four alternative ways to protect against liens being filed against your home. This subject is discussed in detail in Section E above. Normally the first or second approach is the best, but one of the others may prove more suitable to your particular circumstances.

But be warned, contractors may balk at this clause. After all, it deprives the contractor of an important protection and complicates his or her relationship with subcontractors and suppliers of materials. If you decide not to use this clause, do your best to make sure that the contractor has paid the materials supplier and the subcontractors, and that the work is done to your satisfaction, before you make the final payment. Also, write: ***Final payment for labor and materials under contract signed (date)*** on the check.

9. *Materials*

It is important to specify the materials that will be used in the work. This means a literal description and the grade of material.

For example, materials for a new deck might include:

Joists, ledger and beam. No. 2 or better Douglas fir.
4" X 4" beam supports and railing posts Rd. Construction heart.
2" X 12" facia Rd. Con. heart.
2" X 6" decking facia grade redwood.
2" X 4" & 2" X 2" railing material select heart redwood.
All hardware, joist hangers and 16d screw nails galvanized.
Tops of joists and ledger to have flashing.

These contracts require that all materials be new and of generally recognized high quality, except where indicated otherwise. This exception recognizes that in some instances used or lower grade materials will be suitable, so long as they are specifically agreed upon. If the specific materials to be used are already included in the description of the work in Clause 1 or in an attachment to Clause 1, refer to that here. Otherwise, attach a schedule of materials to the contract and indicate that in the blank.

In most moderate home repairs, the contractor will obtain the materials as part of the job. However, it is possible that the homeowner has better access to the necessary materials than the contractor—perhaps through a friend or relative—and will arrange for their purchase. If you are responsible for obtaining the materials, specify that in Clause 9.

10. What Constitutes Completion

It's very important to agree in advance on how to tell when the job is done. This clause provides that completion is subject to the homeowner's approval but that such approval may not be unreasonably withheld. What this means is that the contractor must get paid unless the homeowner's disapproval has a reasonable basis. If the homeowner refuses to give his approval and the contractor believes that this refusal is unreasonable, the contractor can invoke one of the remedies provided for in Clause 12. This issue is discussed more fully in Section G (What to Do If The Contract Is Broken).

11. Limited warranties

In moderate home repairs, it is common for the contractor to guarantee that the job will be carried out in a workmanlike manner consistent with recognized standards for the trade and that all work will comply with state and local building codes and regulations. It is also common for the contractor to guarantee or warrant that the work and materials will hold up for a period of time—often a year. We provide some standard warranty language to accomplish these goals and also leave you room to describe any additional warranty that the contractor may be offering. For instance, the contractor may offer a ten year warranty for a roof in addition to the general one year warranty provided for in the clause. Or a the contractor may offer a special three year warranty on the finish applied to a deck.

12. Dispute Resolution

This form provides for a several step process to resolve any disputes that you and the contractor may have under the contract. The process starts with mediation, which is designed to help you and the contractor settle your dispute without the need for a judge or arbitrator to impose a solution. If a party refuses to cooperate or the mediation doesn't work, the next step will be either arbitration, small claims court, or regular court, depending on which option you and the contractor select. (See Section G for a discussion of these options.)

If attorneys are required, this contract allows you to choose whether each party should pay his or her own attorney fees, or whether the loser should pay the winner's.

13. Additional Agreements and Amendments

This clause allows you to describe other agreements you and the contractor have reached. For instance, if you own a farm, you may want to be more specific about when drills and saws can be used since noise can interrupt important routines. Or if you are allergic to certain substances, you may want to specify that they not be used.

Also, you may wish to add information to one or more of the clauses already written in the contract. Do so by first writing in: *Contractor and Homeowner add the following language to Clause* ___. Insert the language that describes your additional agreement. Then add this sentence: *This additional language shall apply in case of a conflict between it and existing language in Clause* ___.

For example, you may want to specify that if the job isn't done on time as specified in Clause 3, you will have the right to hire a replacement contractor to finish the job and deduct the additional cost from what you owe the first contractor for work completed. Insert the following language here:

Contractor and Homeowner add the following language to Clause 3: If the time limits in this clause are not met by Contractor, Homeowner shall have the right to hire a replacement contractor and deduct any additional costs from work already completed by contractor. This additional language shall apply in case of a conflict between it and existing language in Clause 2.

If you wish to add additional clauses to this contract, perhaps from one of the other contracts in this chapter, take the following steps:

- Label a blank 8 1/2" by 11" piece of paper "Attachment A".
- Reproduce on Attachment A the clause or clauses you wish to use in this contract, and fill them in.
- Use the following language in this clause to make Attachment A part of this contract: "*Contractor and Homeowner incorporate the clauses set out on Attachment A as if fully set out herein.*"
- Sign or initial (both you and the contractor) each clause on Attachment A.

Finally, the last part of this clause also provides that all agreements between you and the contractor have been made part of this written contract and that any changes in or additions to the contract must be in writing. These provisions prevent either you or the contractor from contradicting the plain terms of this contract by arguing that a separate oral agreement was made before the contract was signed, or that an oral amendment was made to the contract after it was signed.

Contract 4: Extensive Home Repairs or Remodeling

Begin by providing details on the people involved and the location of the home repair work.

a. In the first blank, write in your own name. For the rest of the contract, you will be referred to as "Homeowner."

b. Write in the name of the person who has agreed to do the work—to be called "Contractor" for purposes of the contract.

c. Write in your street address. Include the city, state and zip code.

1. Job Description

For extensive home repairs, a description of the work is likely to be fairly complex. A starting place is the contractor's estimate. This typically will consist of a total amount for labor and materials and separate amounts for each component. The work that will be done by subcontractors will also be broken down and described separately. Upon accepting the job, the contractor will need to prepare a more detailed description—for the purpose of obtaining permits and organizing the task—of what work will be done and when, what materials will be required, and which sub-contractors will be used, if any. Blueprints or illustrations may also be part of the description. After you review, understand and approve the work in these materials, the description can easily be shoehorned into this clause. Write the following:

The services to be performed under this contract are fully set out in Attachment 1 to this agreement, entitled Work Design, which is incorporated in this contract.

Sometimes, homeowners have a general idea of what they want done, but want to maintain control over the pace of the job and selection of the materials. For instance, they may want a sizeable yard landscaped and decked, but don't want to commit to an overall design in advance. In this situation, the contractor may need to proceed in a series of phases, with each phase providing direction for the succeeding phase. If so, the description of the job will have to be general, allowing for successive more detailed descriptions on a phased basis. This contract allows for this type of flexibility.

2. Payment Terms

Contractors who perform extensive home repairs generally get paid for their labor in one of a number of ways:

a. A single amount for the total job, including labor and materials payable in a number of installments—for instance, 10% at the beginning of the job and 20% when specified parts of the job have been completed, another 30% when additional specified work has been completed and 40%

upon final satisfactory completion and approval by owner.[2]

Example: *Contractor agrees to remodel Homeowner's kitchen. The total job will cost $25,000, including labor and materials, payable $2,500 in advance, $5,000 upon removal of the interior separating wall and installation of new dry wall, $7,500 upon installation of the cabinets, and $10,000 upon final completion.*

b. A contract amount for total labor, payable in several installments, plus cost for materials as incurred.

Example: *Contractor agrees to remodel Homeowner's kitchen. The total labor for the kitchen shall run $10,000, $1,000 payable in advance, $5,000 payable when the job is half completed as indicated in the plans, and $4,000 upon completion. Materials shall be paid for by Homeowner at the time of delivery to the worksite.*

c. Time actually spent, periodically billed at an hourly rate, plus cost of materials.

Example: *Contractor agrees to remodel Homeowner's kitchen. Contractor shall biweekly bill Homeowner for time spent, at the rate of $25 an hour to a maximum of $10,000, and for materials purchased and delivered during that period.*

d. For jobs that are to proceed in several phases, an initial amount for the first phase of the job (perhaps half in advance and half upon completion) and additional amounts to be negotiated and put in writing for each successive phase.

Example: *Contractor agrees to remodel Homeowner's kitchen. The work is to proceed in four phases:*

- *Phase one: construction of the new kitchen space, including removal of two walls, and the addition of a bay window and a skylight.*
- *Phase two: plumbing and wiring.*
- *Phase three: custom cabinet work.*
- *Phase four: finish work, including tile, floors, panelling, wall paper.*

Labor and materials for the first phase will be $15,000, payable half in advance and half upon completion. The cost of labor and materials for each succeeding phase shall be subject to separate agreements, which shall be added to this contract as written amendments.

NOTE: Although payment for materials is covered in this clause, Clause 9 describes the materials to be used.

3. Time of Performance

Contracts for extensive home repairs should specify the approximate length of time the work will take. This clause provides a space for you to specify this period of time. Because the work being done under this contract is expected to last two weeks or longer, it is important to decide in advance what will happen if the work is delayed, or unanticipated expenses are incurred. These topics are addressed in Clauses 13 and 14 below.

This clause also provides that "Time is of the essence," which means that you are serious about the times specified in the contract and reserve the right to pursue your remedies under Clauses 13 and 14 if the job isn't completed on time.

---

[2] If your state regulates home repair and contractors, it may limit the amount that can be charged as a down payment. Check with your state's regulatory agency.

4. *Independent Contractor Status*

In this clause you specify that the contractor is an independent contractor and check off the items that support this conclusion. If you aren't able to check most of the items, the chances are excellent that the person is—legally—an employee rather than an independent contractor. Be sure to read Section C of this chapter for a more detailed discussion of what constitutes an independent contractor. Although you can't make an employee into an independent contractor by completing this clause, you can use it to clarify your view of the contractor's legal status.

5. *License Status and Number*

If the work is being done by a plumber, electrician, or a person who advertises as a licensed contractor, use this blank to describe the license by type and number. If a dispute arises as to the quality of the work, you may have some recourse with the state licensing board. See Section D above for a discussion of licensing requirements and potential recourse.

If there is no license requirement for the type of work being done, that box should be checked and reasons provided.

If there is a license requirement but the contractor is unlicensed, skip this clause.

6. *Liability Waiver*

This clause handles the liability issue by making the contractor responsible for his own injuries to the fullest extent possible under the law. (See Section D.3 for a discussion of liability for on-the-job injuries.)

NOTE: If the contractor is using subcontractors or employees, or the work being done risks injuries to neighbors or others, you may wish to also use the indemnification clause (Clause 15). That clause makes the contractor responsible for claims against you by others, and lets you require the Contractor to obtain business liability insurance, listing you as a co-insured, and workers' compensation insurance, if necessary. See the instructions for Clause 18 on how to add clauses to this agreement.

7. *Permits and Approvals*

Because the repairs covered by this contract are extensive, it is likely that a building permit will be required. If that is not the case, simply skip over the clause. (See Section F.2 for a discussion of permits and approvals.)

8. *Liens and Waivers of Liens*

This contract offers four alternative ways to protect against liens being filed against your home. This subject is discussed in detail in Section E above. Normally the first or second approach is the best, but one of the others may prove more suitable to your particular circumstances.

But be warned. Contractors may balk at this clause. After all, it deprives the contractor of an important protection and complicates his or her relationship with subcontractors and suppliers of materials. If you decide not to use this clause, do your best to make sure that the contractor has paid the materials supplier and the subcontractors, and that the work is done to your satisfaction, before you make the final payment. Also, write *Final payment for labor and materials under contract signed (date)* on the check.

9. *Materials*

It is important to specify the materials that will be used in the work. This means a literal description and the grade of material. These contracts require that all materials be new and of generally recognized high quality, except where the parties indicate otherwise. This exception recognizes that in some instances used or lower grade materials will be suitable, so long as they are specifically agreed upon. If the specific materials to be used are already included in the description of the work in Clause 2 or in an attachment to Clause 2, refer to that clause here. Otherwise, attach a schedule of materials to the contract and indicate that in the blank.

In most extensive home repair situations, the contractor will obtain the materials as part of the job. However, it is possible that the homeowner has better access to the necessary materials than the contractor—perhaps through a friend or relative—and will arrange for their purchase. If you are responsible for obtaining the materials, specify that in Clause 9.

10. What Constitutes Completion

It's very important to agree in advance on how to tell when the job is done. This clause provides that completion is subject to the homeowner's approval but that such approval may not be unreasonably withheld. What this means is that the contractor must get paid unless the homeowner's disapproval has a reasonable basis. If the homeowner refuses to give his approval and the contractor believes that this refusal is unreasonable, the contractor can invoke one of the remedies provided for in Clause 12. This issue is discussed more fully in Section G (What to Do If The Contract Is Broken).

11. Limited Warranties

In extensive home repairs or remodeling, it is common for the contractor to guarantee that the job will be carried out in a workmanlike manner consistent with recognized standards for the trade and that all work will comply with state and local building codes and regulations. It is also common for the contractor to guarantee or warrant that the work and materials will hold up for a period of time—often a year. We provide some standard warranty language to accomplish these goals and also leave you room to describe any additional warranty that the contractor may be offering. For instance, the contractor may offer a ten-year warranty for a roof of in addition to the general one-year warranty provided for in the clause. Or a the contractor may offer a special three-year warranty on the finish applied to a deck.

12. Dispute Resolution

This form provides for a several step process to resolve any disputes that you and the contractor may have under the contract. The process starts with mediation, which is designed to help you and the contractor settle your dispute without the need for a judge or arbitrator to impose a solution. If the other side refuses to cooperate or the mediation doesn't work, the next step will be either arbitration, small claims court, or regular court, depending on which option you and the contractor select. (These options are discussed in Section G.)

13. Late Performance

If the contract contains only an approximate completion date, there is normally precious little that the homeowner can do about late performance, assuming the provider shows signs of eventually completing the job. To deal with this problem, Clause 3 states that "Time is of the essence." This clause means that the performance and completion dates in the contract are a very important part of the contract and that lateness will be considered a serious breach of the contract, allowing you to avoid payment.

This kind of clause, of course, is particularly important when timing really does matter. For example, if you contract to have your roof fixed before the rainy season begins and specify that "Time is of the essence," and performance is completed in the middle of the third big storm, you may be up to your ankles in water but at least you won't have to pay the roofer the complete contract price. You may, however, have to pay for work already completed, offset by damages caused by the late performance.

If the damage you are likely to suffer as a result of the contractor's late performance can be fairly estimated in advance in terms of dollars and cents, then the contract may also set out an amount of damages for each day or week the performance is late. This contract offers this option.

14. Change Orders (Mid-Performance Amendments)

Despite the best laid plans, extensive home repairs can sometimes get tangled up in unanticipated events. A shortage of materials may suddenly arise, sub-contractors may strike, supplies may arrive late (for instance, special-order windows) or very unusual weather may intervene. Then too, you may change your mind in the middle of the job and want modifications that will take longer and cost more than the original contract amount.

In these and similar situations, you and the contractor may want to renegotiate some parts of this contract—such as completion dates, labor and material costs, or types of materials to be used—to fit the changed conditions. Although you may be tempted to stick to the terms of the contract as written, this is not recommended if the contractor truly has good reason for wanting the changes. And the contractor would not be wise to refuse your requested changes if they can be reasonably accommodated in the scope of the job. Few courts strictly hold to an original contract if changed circumstances and principles of fairness require reasonable modifications.

15. Indemnification (Hold Harmless) Clause

We discuss indemnification in Section H above. The first part of this indemnification clause shifts responsibility for injuries and damages caused to third parties onto the contractor and away from the homeowner. The second part, if checked, obligates the contractor to obtain adequate liability insurance. You can use either part, or both.

16. Surety Bond

Section D explains that some states require their contractors to maintain a bond as a type of protection against shoddy work or failing to finish a job. Once again, a bond is simply a promise by a third party—the bonding company—that you will be paid a certain amount if the one covered by the bond—the contractor—defaults in meeting his or her legal obligations under the contract. The contractor has to pay for that promise, which is ultimately passed on to consumers twice—in the prices the contractor charges, and as a tax-deductible business expense.

If the contractor already has a bond, then it should be identified in this blank. But if the contractor is not bonded, you may wish to require one. If so, check the box, and fill in the blank when the bond is obtained. Bonding is a very common requirement in the construction trades, and if the contractor balks at this requirement, you may want to find someone else.

17. Site Maintenance (hours, cleanup, noise, areas)

When a homeowner decides to initiate such large projects as adding a bathroom, remodeling the kitchen, or converting the garage into a family room, the work has the potential to seriously disrupt the daily routine of people living in the house—for instance, excessive noise, dust, clutter, inconvenient storage of contractor's equipment, or the temporary dismantling of necessary facilities. In these situations, the contract should specify what behavior by the contractor is and is not acceptable. If your bathroom is being remodeled, your contract might specify that the bathtub, toilet and sink be left operational at the end of each day's work and that the contractor clean up debris daily. Or, if there will be excessive noise on the job, you might negotiate to have the noisy aspects of the job done only during certain hours.

18. Additional Agreements and Amendments

This clause allows you to describe other agreements you and the contractor have reached. For instance, if you own a farm, you may want to be more specific about when drills and saws can be used, since the noise could interrupt important routines. Or if you are allergic to certain substances, you may want to specify that they not be used.

Also, you may wish to add information to one or more of the clauses already written into the contract by first writing in: *Contractor and Homeowner add the following language to Clause ___*. Insert the language that describes your additional agreement. Then add this sentence: *This additional language shall apply in case of a conflict between it and existing language in Clause ____*.

For example, assume you may want to specify that if the job isn't done on time as specified in Clause 3, you will have the right to hire a replacement contractor to finish the job and deduct the additional cost from what you owe the first contractor for work completed. Insert the following language in this clause:

Contractor and Homeowner add the following language to Clause 3: If the time limits in this clause are not met by Contractor, Homeowner shall have the right to hire a replacement contractor and deduct any additional costs from work already completed by Contractor. This additional language shall apply in case of a conflict between it and existing language in Clause 2.

If you wish to add additional clauses to this contract, perhaps from one of the other contracts in this chapter, take the following steps:

- Label a blank 8 1/2" by 11" piece of paper "Attachment A".
- Reproduce on Attachment A the clause or clauses you wish to use in this contract, and fill them in.
- Use the following language in this clause to make Attachment A part of this contract: *Contractor and Homeowner incorporate the clauses set out on Attachment A as if fully set out herein.*
- Sign or initial (both you and the contractor) each clause on Attachment A.

Finally, the last part of the clause also provides that all agreements between you and the contractor have been made part of this written contract and that any changes in or additions to the contract must be in writing. These provisions prevent either you or the contractor from contradicting the plain terms of this contract by arguing that a separate oral agreement was made before the contract was signed, or that an oral amendment was made to the contract after it was signed.

CONTRACT FOR HOME MAINTENANCE

______________________________, Homeowner, desires to contract with,

______________________________, Contractor, to perform certain work

on property located at : ______________________________

____

1. Job Description

The work to be performed under this agreement consists of the following: ______________________________

____

____

____

____

____

____

2. Payment Terms

In exchange for the specified work, Homeowner agrees to pay Contractor as follows (choose one and check the appropriate boxes):

☐ a. $ ______________, payable upon completion of the specified work by ☐ cash ☐ check.

☐ b. $ ______________, payable one half at the beginning of the specified work and one half at the completion of the specified work by ☐ cash ☐ check.

☐ c. $ ______________ per hour for each hour of work performed, up to a maximum of $ ______________, payable at the following times and in the following manner: ______________________________

____

____

3. Time of Performance

The work specified in this contract shall (check the boxes and provide dates):

☐ begin on ______________________________

☐ be completed on ______________________________

4. Independent Contractor Status

It is agreed that Contractor shall perform the specified work as an independent contractor. Contractor (check the appropriate boxes and provide description, if necessary):

☐ maintains his or her own independent business.

☐ shall use his or her own tools and equipment except: ______________________________

____

____

☐ shall perform the work specified in Clause 1 independent of Homeowner's supervision, being responsible only for satisfactory completion of the work.

5. Additional Agreements and Amendments

a. Homeowner and Contractor additionally agree that: ______________________________

____

____

____

____

b. All agreements between Homeowner and Contractor related to the specified work are incorporated in this contract. Any modification to the contract shall be in writing.

Homeowner: ______________________________ Dated: ______________

Contractor: ______________________________ Dated: ______________

CONTRACT FOR SIMPLE HOME REPAIRS

______________________________, Homeowner, desires to contract with,

______________________________, Contractor, to perform certain work

on property located at : ______________________________

____

1. Job Description

The work to be performed under this agreement consists of the following: ______________________________

____

____

____

____

____

____

2. Payment Terms

In exchange for the specified work, Homeowner agrees to pay Contractor as follows (choose one and check the appropriate boxes):

☐ a. $ ____________, payable upon completion of the specified work by ☐ cash ☐ check.

☐ b. $ ____________, payable one half at the beginning of the specified work and one half at the completion of the specified work by ☐ cash ☐ check.

☐ c. $ ____________ per hour for each hour of work performed, up to a maximum of $ ____________, payable at the following times and in the following manner: ______________________________

____

____

3. Time of Performance

The work specified in this contract shall (check the boxes and provide dates):

☐ begin on ______________________________

☐ be completed on ______________________________

Time is of the essence.

4. Independent Contractor Status

It is agreed that Contractor shall perform the specified work as an independent contractor. Contractor (check one box and provide description, if necessary):

☐ maintains his or her own independent business.

☐ shall use his or her own tools and equipment except: ______________________________

____

____

☐ shall perform the work specified in Clause 1 independent of Homeowner's supervision, being responsible only for satisfactory completion of the work.

5. License Status and Number

Contractor shall comply with all state and local licensing and registration requirements for type of activity involved in the specified work.

(Check one box and provide description)

☐ Contractor's state license or registration is for the following type of work and carries the following number: __________

____

____

☐ Contractor's local license or registration is for the following type of work and carries the following number: __________

____

____

☐ Contractor is not required to have a license or registration for the specified work, for the following reasons: __________

____

____

6. Liability Waiver

If Contractor is injured in the course of performing the specified work, Homeowner shall be exempt from liability for those injuries to the fullest extent allowed by law.

7. Permits and Approvals

(Check the appropriate boxes)

☐ Contractor ☐ Homeowner shall be responsible for determining which permits are necessary and for obtaining the permits.

☐ Contractor ☐ Homeowner shall pay for all state and local permits necessary for performing the specified work.

☐ Contractor ☐ Homeowner shall be responsible for obtaining approval from the local homeowner's association, if required.

8. Additional Agreements and Amendments

a. Homeowner and Contractor additionally agree that: ____

____

____

____

____

____

____

b. All agreements between Homeowner and Contractor related to the specified work are incorporated in this contract. Any modification to the contract shall be in writing.

Homeowner: ______________________________________ Dated: ____________________

Contractor: ______________________________________ Dated: ____________________

CONTRACT FOR MODERATE HOME REPAIRS

____, Homeowner, desires to contract with,

____, Contractor, to perform certain work

on property located at : ____

____

1. Job Description

The work to be performed under this agreement consists of the following: ______________________

____

____

____

____

____

____

2. Payment Terms

In exchange for the specified work, homeowner agrees to pay Contractor as follows (choose one, check the appropriate boxes and provide description):

☐ a. $______________, payable upon completion of the specified work for all labor and materials by ☐ cash ☐ check.

☐ b. $______________, payable for labor upon completion of the specified work by ☐ cash ☐ check. Materials shall be paid for by Homeowner upon their delivery to the worksite, or as follows: ______________

____

____

☐ c. $______________, payable for all labor and materials in installments as follows ☐ cash ☐ check:

____

____

☐ d. $______________, payable in installments for labor by ☐ cash ☐ check as follows: ______________

____

____

Materials shall be paid for by Homeowner upon their delivery to the worksite, or as follows: ______________

____

____

____

☐ e. $ ____________________, per hour for each hour of work performed, up to a maximum of $ ____________________

____ payable at the following times and in the following manner:

____

____

3. Time of Performance

The specified work shall (check the boxes and provide dates):

☐ begin on ____

☐ be completed no later than ____

Time is of the essence.

4. Independent Contractor Status

It is agreed that Contractor shall perform the specified work as an independent contractor. Contractor (check one box and provide description, if necessary):

☐ maintains his or her own independent business.

☐ shall use his or her own tools, except: ____

____

____

____

☐ shall perform the specified work independent of Homeowner's supervision, being responsible only for satisfactory completion of the work as specified in Clause 1.

5. License Status and Number

Contractor shall comply with all state and local licensing and registration requirements for type of work involved in Clause 1. (check one box and provide description):

☐ Contractor's state license or registration is for the following type of work and carries the following number: ____________

____

____

☐ Contractor's local license or registration is for the following type of work and carries the following number: ____________

____

____

☐ Contractor is not required to have a license or registration for the specified work, for the following reasons: ____________

____

____

6. Liability Waiver

If Contractor is injured while performing the specified work, Homeowner shall be exempt from liability for such injuries to the fullest extent allowed by law.

7. Permits and Permissions

[Check the appropriate boxes]

☐ Contractor ☐ Homeowner shall be responsible for determining which permits are necessary and for obtaining the permits.

☐ Contractor ☐ Homeowner shall pay for all state and local permits necessary for performing the specified work.

☐ Contractor ☐ Homeowner shall be responsible for obtaining permission from the local homeowner's association, if required.

8. Liens and Waivers of Liens

To protect Homeowner against liens being filed by Contractor, subcontractors and providers of materials, Contractor agrees that (check one box and provide description, if necessary):

☐ a. Final payment to Contractor under Clause 2 shall be withheld by Homeowner until Contractor presents Homeowner with lien waivers, lien releases, or acknowledgment of full payment from each subcontractor and materials provider.

☐ b. All checks to Contractor shall also be made out jointly to all subcontractors and materials suppliers.

☐ c. Contractor shall not:

- use a subcontractor without first obtaining a lien waiver or release and delivering a copy to Homeowner; or
- use any materials without obtaining an "acknowledgment of full payment" from the materials supplier and delivering a copy to Homeowner.

☐ d. Homeowner and Contractor agree that Homeowner shall be protected against liens in the following manner: ____________

____

____

____

9. Materials

a. All materials shall be new, of good quality, in compliance with all applicable laws and codes, and shall be covered by a manufacturer's warranty if appropriate, except as follows: ______________________________

____

____

____

____

b. The materials shall consist of (check one box and provide description, if necessary):

☐ the materials described in Clause 1.

☐ the materials described in the Schedule of Materials attached to this contract.

☐ the following items:____

c. The materials shall be purchased by (check one box):

☐ Contractor, to be reimbursed as specified in Clause 2.

☐ Homeowner.

10. What Constitutes Completion

The specified work shall be considered completed upon approval by Homeowner, provided that Homeowner's approval shall not be unreasonably withheld. Substantial performance of the specified work in a workmanlike manner shall be considered sufficient grounds for Contractor to require final payment by Homeowner, except as provided in Clause 8 (Liens and Waivers of Liens).

11. Limited Warranties

Contractor will complete the specified work in a substantial and workmanlike manner according to standard practices prevalent in Contractor's trade. Contractor warrants that:

[Check one or more boxes and provide descriptions, if necessary]

☐ the specified work will comply with all applicable building codes and regulations.

☐ the labor and materials provided as part of the specified work will be free from defects for ____________________ from the date of completion.

☐ Additional warranties offered by the Contractor are as follows: ____________________________

____

____

____

12. Dispute Resolution

If any dispute arises under the terms of this agreement, the parties agree to select a mutually agreeable neutral third party to help them mediate it. If the mediation is deemed unsuccessful, the parties agree that (check one box):

☐ the dispute shall be decided by the applicable small claims court if the amount in dispute is within the court's jurisdiction, and otherwise by binding arbitration under the rules issued by the American Arbitration Association. The decision of the arbitrator shall be final.

☐ the dispute shall be directly submitted to binding arbitration under the rules issued by the American Arbitration Association. The decision of the arbitrator shall be final.

☐ the dispute shall be settled according to the laws of the state that apply to this agreement.

Any costs and fees (other than attorney fees) associated with mediation and arbitration shall be shared equally by the parties.

Attorney fees associated with arbitration or litigation shall be paid as follows (check one box):

☐ Each party shall pay his or her own attorney fees.

☐ The reasonable attorney fees of the prevailing party shall be paid by the other party.

13. Additional Agreements and Amendments

a. Homeowner and Contractor additionally agree that: ______________________________

____

____

____

____

____

____

____

____

b. All agreements between Homeowner and Contractor related to the specified work are incorporated in this contract. Any modification to the contract shall be in writing.

Homeowner: ______________________________ Dated: ______________

Contractor: ______________________________ Dated: ______________

CONTRACT FOR EXTENSIVE HOME REPAIRS OR REMODELING

_______________________________, Homeowner, desires to contract with,

_______________________________, Contractor, to perform certain work

on property located at : _______________________________

____

1. Job Description

The work to be performed under this agreement consists of the following: _______________

____

____

____

____

____

____

2. Payment Terms

In exchange for the specified work, homeowner agrees to pay Contractor as follows (choose one, check the appropriate boxes and provide description):

☐ a. $ _______________, payable for all labor and materials, in installments by ☐ cash ☐ check as follows:

____

____

____

☐ b. $ _______________, payable in installments for labor by ☐ cash ☐ check as follows: _______

____

____

____

Materials shall be paid for by Homeowner upon their delivery to the worksite, or as follows: _______

____

____

☐ c. $ ____________ per hour for each hour of work performed up to a maximum of $ ____________

plus cost of materials to be billed by Contractor as follows: ____________

____

____

☐ d. $ ____________ including labor and materials for the first phase of the specified work;

$ ____________ payable by ☐ cash ☐ check at the beginning of the specified work;

and $ ____________ payable by ☐ cash ☐ check at completion of the first phase of the specified work. Terms for additional phases of the specified work shall be agreed upon by Contractor and Homeowner prior to the beginning of each additional phase and added to this contract as a written amendment.

3. Time of Performance

The work specified in Clause 1 shall be (check the appropriate boxes and provide dates):

☐ started on or about ____________

☐ completed on or about ____________

☐ started and completed as follows: ____________

____

Time is of the essence.

4. Independent Contractor Status

It is agreed that Contractor shall perform the specified work as an independent contractor. Contractor (check the appropriate boxes and provide description, if necessary):

☐ maintains his or her own independent business.

☐ shall use his or her own tools, except: ____________

____

____

☐ shall perform the specified work independent of Homeowner's supervision, being responsible only for satisfactory completion of the work.

Contractor may use subcontractors, but shall be solely responsible for supervising their work and for the quality of the work they produce.

5. License Status and Number

Contractor shall comply with all state and local licensing and registration requirements for type of work involved (check one box and provide description):

☐ Contractor's state license or registration is for the following type of work and carries the following number: ____________

____

____

☐ Contractor's local license or registration is for the following type of work and carries the following number: ____________

____

____

☐ Contractor is not required to have a license or registration for the Job described in this contract for the following reasons: ____

____

____

6. Liability Waiver

If Contractor is injured in the course of performing the specified work, Homeowner shall be exempt from liability for such injuries to the fullest extent allowed by law.

7. Permits and Approvals

(Check the appropriate boxes)

☐ Contractor ☐ Homeowner shall pay for all state and local permits necessary for performing the specified work.

☐ Contractor ☐ Homeowner shall be responsible for determining which permits are necessary and for obtaining the permits.

☐ Contractor ☐ Homeowner shall be responsible for obtaining permission from the local homeowner's association, if required.

8. Liens and Waivers of Liens

To protect Homeowner against liens being filed by Contractor, subcontractors and providers of materials, Contractor agrees that (check one box and provide description, if necessary):

☐ Final payment to Contractor under Clause 2 shall be withheld by Homeowner until Contractor presents Homeowner with lien waivers, lien releases, or acknowledgment of full payment from each subcontractor and materials provider.

☐ All checks to Contractor shall also be made out jointly to all subcontractors and materials suppliers.

☐ Contractor shall not:

- use a subcontractor without first obtaining a lien waiver or release and delivering a copy to Homeowner; or
- use any materials without obtaining an "acknowledgment of full payment" from the materials supplier and delivering a copy to Homeowner.

☐ Homeowner and Contractor agree that Homeowner shall be protected against liens in the following manner: ____________

____

____

____

9. Materials

All materials shall be new, in compliance with all applicable laws and codes, and shall be covered by a manufacturer's warranty if appropriate, except as follows: ______

The materials shall consist of (check one box and provide description, if necessary):

☐ the materials described in Clause 1.

☐ the materials described in the Schedule of Materials attached to this contract.

☐ the following items: ______

____

____

The materials shall be purchased by (check one box):

☐ Contractor, to be reimbursed as provided in Clause 2.

☐ Homeowner

10. What Constitutes Completion

The work specified in Clause 1 shall be considered completed upon approval by Homeowner, provided that Homeowner's approval shall not be unreasonably withheld. Substantial performance of the specified work in a workmanlike manner shall be considered sufficient grounds for Contractor to require final payment by Homeowner, except as provided in Clause 8 (Liens and Waivers of Liens).

11. Limited Warranties

Contractor will complete the specified work in a substantial and workmanlike manner according to standard practices prevalent in Contractor's trade. Contractor warrants that (check the appropriate boxes and provide descriptions, if necessary):

☐ the specified work shall comply with all applicable building codes and regulations.

☐ the labor and materials provided as part of the specified work shall be free from defects for ____________________ from the date of completion of the work.

☐ Additional warranties offered by the Contractor are as follows: ______________________________________

____

____

____

____

____

12. Dispute Resolution

If any dispute arises under the terms of this agreement, the parties agree to select a mutually agreeable neutral third party to help them mediate it. If the mediation is deemed unsuccessful, the parties agree that (check one box):

☐ the dispute shall be decided by the applicable small claims (or comparable) court if the amount in dispute is within the court's jurisdiction, and otherwise by binding arbitration under the rules issued by the American Arbitration Association. The decision of the arbitrator shall be final.

☐ the dispute shall be directly submitted to binding arbitration under the rules issued by the American Arbitration Association. The decision of the arbitrator shall be final.

☐ the dispute shall be settled according to the laws of the state that apply to this agreement.

Any costs and fees (other than attorney fees) associated with mediation and arbitration shall be shared equally by the parties.

Attorney fees associated with arbitration or litigation shall be paid as follows (check one box):

☐ Each party shall pay his or her own attorney fees.

☐ The reasonable attorney fees of the prevailing party shall be paid by the other party.

13. Late Performance

If performance of the specified work is late, Contractor agrees that (check one box and provide description, if necessary):

☐ Homeowner shall be damaged in the amount of $____________________ per ________________________________,
and that Contractor shall be liable for such sums, which may be credited against any sums owed to Contractor by Homeowner.

☐ A dispute over any damages or loss claimed by Homeowner for the delay in performance of the specified work shall be resolved as provided in Clause 12 of this agreement.

14. Change Orders (Mid-Performance Amendments)

The Contractor and Homeowner recognize that:

- Contractor's original cost and time estimates may prove too low due to unforeseen events, or to factors unknown to the Contractor when the contract was made;
- Homeowner may desire a mid-job change in the specifications that would add time and cost to the specified work and possibly inconvenience the Contractor; or
- Other provisions of the contract may be difficult to carry out because of unforeseen events, such as a materials shortage or a labor strike.

If these or other events beyond the control of the parties reasonably require adjustments to this contract, the parties shall make a good faith attempt to agree on all necessary particulars. Such agreements shall be put in writing, signed by the parties and added to this contract. Failure to reach agreement shall be deemed a dispute to be resolved as agreed in Clause 12.

15. Indemnification (Hold Harmless) Clause

Contractor agrees to (check appropriate boxes and provide description, if necessary):

☐ Hold harmless and indemnify Homeowner for all damages, costs and attorney fees that arise out of harm caused to Contractor, subcontractors and other third parties, known and unknown, by Contractor's performance of the specified work, except as follows: ____

____

____

☐ Obtain adequate business liability insurance that will cover Job and any injuries to subcontractors or employees.

16. Surety Bond

Prior to beginning job, Contractor shall be required to obtain a surety bond covering Contractor's obligations under this contract, in the amount of $ ______________________ .

17. Site Maintenance

Contractor agrees to be bound by the following conditions when performing the specified work (check the appropriate boxes and provide descriptions):

☐ Contractor shall perform the specified work between the following hours: ______________________

____

____

☐ At the end of each day's work, Contractor's equipment shall be stored in the following location: ______________________

____

____

☐ At the end of each day's work, Contractor agrees to clean all debris from the work area and leave all appliances and facilities in good working order except as follows: ______________________

____

____

☐ Contractor agrees that disruptively loud activities shall be performed only at the following times: ______________________

____

____

☐ Contractor agrees to confine all work-related activity, materials and products, including dust and debris, to the following areas:

____

____

☐ Contractor agrees that: ______________________

____

____

____

____

____

18. Additional Agreements and Amendments

a. Homeowner and Contractor additionally agree that: ______________________

____

____

____

____

____

____

____

____

____

____

b. All agreements between Homeowner and Contractor related to the work specified in Clause 1 are incorporated in this contract. Any modification to the contract shall be in writing.

Homeowner: ____ Dated: ______________________

Contractor: ____ Dated: ______________________

Chapter 7

In-Home Child Care and Other Household Help

Many people hire others to work regularly in their homes—for example, to take care of their children during the workday or clean their houses. These relationships are often set up informally, with no written agreement and paid for in cash, "off the books."

But such informal arrangements can be fraught with problems. If you don't have a written agreement clearly defining responsibilities and benefits, you and your employee may have different expectations about the job. This can lead to serious disputes—even to either or both of you bitterly backing out of the arrangement.

A. The Value of a Written Contract

We can't advise you on how to choose high-quality child care or other household help, although we suggest some useful resources in this chapter. But we can help assure a successful arrangement by providing two sample written agreements—one for child care and one for housecleaning services. By drafting and discussing a proposed contract *before* you hire someone, you'll both clearly define your needs and expectations and assure a longer and better relationship. And even if you choose not to put your agreement in writing, this discussion can help ward off problems and misunderstandings with your child care provider or household employee.

1. Child Care Options

The type of child care you choose depends on many factors—the age and number of your children, your budget, work schedule, location, personal and educational philosophy and household needs.

If you take your children to a family day care home or a day care center, written contracts will not usually be appropriate, because the care—including fees, hours and type of program—is not tailored to your individual child but is set by the provider.

Written contracts are extremely useful, however, for in-home child care because you can specify the schedule, payment, benefits and type of care and there is generally a single child care provider.

A child care provider who takes care of your children in your house, either part-time or full-time may live out (often called a care giver or babysitter) or live in (an au pair or nanny). The responsibilities of the position may vary widely, from performing a wide range of housekeeping services to only taking care of the children.

RESOURCES

The Complete Guide to Choosing Child Care by Judith Berezin and the National Association of Child Care Resource and Referral Agencies, Random House. This excellent book won't find the perfect child care provider for you, but gives solid, well-organized information to decide what type of care you need, how to find it, and most important, how to judge if it's truly excellent.

Your local child care resource and referral agency, such as Bananas in Berkeley, California or Child Care, Inc. in New York City, offer a wide range of information and referrals to individual and group child care arrangements and agencies placing au pairs and nannies. There are more than two hundred local agencies throughout the country. For the nearest one, contact the National Association of Child Care Resource and Referral Agencies in Rochester, Minnesota at (507) 287-2020. Your state child care licensing agency may also refer you to a local resource agency.

2. Housecleaning Services

If you hire the same person every week to clean your house, a written contract can be a valuable way to clearly define the worker's responsibilities and benefits. Your basic contract should cover regular weekly tasks—for example, cleaning the bathrooms—while special projects such as washing blinds and ironing curtains may require a separate agreement or a special addition to the contract if you want them completed regularly.

A regular housecleaner who has his or her own business or works for a large firm will probably come complete with a prewritten contract; in this case, our agreement will be useful as a checklist of key issues.

B. The Legal Status of Household Help

If you are paying an individual to work in your home on a daily or regular basis—whether a full-time babysitter or a cleaning person who comes in several times at regular intervals—first decide whether the worker is legally considered to be an employee or an independent contractor. In the following discussion, we explain why most household workers are employees and what this means in terms of your legal obligations.

Federal and state agencies define whether a particular worker is an independent contractor or an employee. The IRS alone sets out 20 factors in making this decision, not all of which have to be satisfied. Most states have a threshold amount of wages paid and number of hours worked—for example, 60 hours a quarter—which trigger a worker's classification as an employee.

The law tilts toward classifying workers as employees for a relatively simple reason: Employees provide the primary funding for government programs set up to protect workers—for example, Social Security and unemployment insurance. The more workers are characterized as employees (whose benefits are paid for by their employers), the more solvent the government programs. Independent contractors, on the other hand, don't receive benefits accorded employees and don't contribute to the benefit funds.

Here are some of the main ways an independent contractor and an employee differ:

INDEPENDENT CONTRACTOR	EMPLOYEE
Supervision Works free from supervision of the person paying for the services, responsible only for the final result	**Supervision** The employer provides instructions on what work must be done and how to do the work
Benefits Typically does not receive benefits. Responsible for paying his or her own Social Security and taxes	**Benefits** Employer is responsible for Social Security (which may be split with employee), workers' compensation, unemployment and disability insurance. Employer may give other benefits as well
Number of Employers Offers services to the public at large, not to just one person or company—for example, has a business license or advertises services	**Number of Employers** Usually works for one or two employers
Method of Payment Contract amount for job or hourly rate, usually not a continuing relationship	**Method of Payment** Typically paid a salary or hourly wage, and works at a job for an indefinite time, under the schedule or routine established by employer
Equipment and Supplies Supplies own equipment and supplies and has own business at a definite location	**Equipment and Supplies** Employer provides equipment and supplies and a place to work. Employee does not maintain a discrete business office or location

For More Information: For the specific IRS definitions of independent contractor and employee, see IRS Form SS8. Contact your state's department of employment or labor standards for state definitions which may be more restrictive.

Most in-home child care providers and other regular domestic help are employees—rather than independent contractors—because you set the hours, the responsibilities, benefits and pay rate.

Your child care provider, for example, must usually comply with your instructions about when, where and how to work. For example, a babysitter who comes to your house weekdays from 8 A.M. to 6 P.M., follows your directions for feeding, bathing, and taking care of your infant and is paid by the hour, week or month rather than by the job will legally be considered an employee.

The person who regularly cleans your house will also usually be an employee. This is because of the ongoing nature is your supervision and the fact that, in most cases, he or she will be using your tools, such as a vacuum cleaner. If your housecleaner is self-employed, has her own business and brings her own vacuum cleaner and cleaning supplies to your house, she would probably be considered an independent contractor, rather than an employee. (Chapter 6, Section 7 includes a more detailed discussion of whether a person working in your home can qualify as an independent contractor.)

UNDOCUMENTED WORKERS

Many babysitters, au pairs and household employees work illegally—that is, they are not U.S. citizens and they don't have a "green card" or other documentation of their legal status. The federal government is deporting an increasing number of illegal workers and now requires employers to complete a form verifying that an employee is eligible to work, based on the employee providing a copy of a driver's license, Social Security card, or green card.

Form I-9, available from the U.S. Department of Justice Immigration and Naturalization Service (INS), must be signed by both employer and employee, and there are substantial fines for failing to complete this form. Contact the INS at (800) 755-0777 for more detailed information. Be sure to inquire about any federally-authorized programs or special visas for au pairs and nannies which the INS introduces from time to time.

You should also be aware that homeowner's insurance protection may not cover damage or injury related to the actions of an illegal worker. If, for example, a neighbor's child is injured in your home while under the care of an illegal au pair, your insurance company will probably deny coverage of the injury.

C. Employer Responsibilities to Household Workers

When you employ a child care worker or housecleaner, you have specific legal obligations to them. You also become responsible for a certain amount of paperwork and recordkeeping.

1. Social Security and Income Taxes

If you pay a babysitter or housecleaner more than $50 in a three-month period, you must make quarterly Social Security payments on those wages and withhold the employee's share of Social Security.

You do not have to deduct income taxes from wages paid to a household employee for working in your home, unless he or she requests that you make the deduction and you agree to do so. Whether or not you withhold income taxes, you must still provide employees with a W-2 form (*Wage and Tax Statement*) for the previous year's earnings by January 31. An employee who wants you to withhold federal income tax must give you a completed W-4 form (*Employee Withholding Allowance Certificate*).

The following resources will help you figure out and fulfill your Social Security and federal tax obligations. To get these materials, call the IRS at 800-TAX-FORM:

- *Employment Taxes for Household Employers* (Publication 926), which describes the major tax responsibilities of employers
- *Employer's Tax Guide* (Circular E), for federal income tax withholding tables
- *Employer's Quarterly Tax Return for Household Employees* (Form 942), for use in reporting Social Security taxes and any federal income tax withheld
- *Child and Dependent Care Expenses* (Publication 503), which explains the requirements you must meet to claim a child care tax credit.

Contact your state's department of labor or the government agency which oversees your state income tax program for state tax requirements.

2. Unemployment Compensation

If you pay a household employee $1,000 or more in wages in a three-month period, you must pay annual taxes in accord with the Federal Unemployment Tax Act (FUTA), using IRS Form 940 or 940-EZ. In most states, you will also be responsible for state unemployment taxes; you can usually credit your federal unemployment tax against these. Contact a nearby state unemployment office for information on state requirements.

3. Workers' Compensation

Your state may require you to provide workers' compensation insurance against job-related injuries or illnesses suffered by your employees. Ask your insurance agent if your homeowner's or renter's insurance policy covers workers' compensation for your babysitter or household help or whether you need to purchase an additional policy. Your state department of employment or labor standards may also operate a workers' compensation insurance fund from which you can purchase coverage.

HELP WITH PAPERWORK

For those of you who hate paperwork, keep in mind that there are many outside payroll services that will handle virtually all the details of employing a child care worker or housecleaner—for example, withholding Social Security and unemployment taxes—for a relatively small fee, such as $20 to $50 per month. To get cost quotes, check the yellow pages under Payroll Service or Bookkeeping Service.

4. Minimum Wage

Federal laws set the minimum hourly wage at $4.25. And your child care and other household workers may be entitled to minimum wage and overtime, depending upon their particular responsibilities, hours and earnings. Contact your state department of labor for specific information.

REALITY CHECK

Many families don't contribute to either taxes or Social Security for household workers and many people hire undocumented workers. This chapter is not intended to preach about the law, but to alert you to the legal controls on your relationships with child care and domestic workers.

If you don't pay Social Security and meet your other legal obligations as an employer, there may be several negative consequences:

- You may be assessed substantial financial penalties. For example, if your full-time babysitter files for Social Security five years from now and can prove prior earnings, but no Social Security has been paid, the IRS could back-bill you at high interest rates.
- If you don't have workers' compensation insurance, and your child care worker breaks a leg while on the job and can't work for a few months, you may be in hot water if he or she files for workers' compensation. You will probably be held liable for the worker's medical costs and a portion of her lost wages, as well as be fined for not having the insurance in the first place.
- If you are a parent, you will not be able to take a child care tax credit on your federal income taxes. The credit is based on your work-related expenses and income, with a maximum of $2,400 per child and $4,800 for two or more children.

D. Instructions for Completing the Contracts

1. Child Care

Your written agreement should clearly specify your employee's responsibilities, hours, benefits, form and schedule of payment and termination policy. The more responsibilities you give your child care worker, the more you will have to fill out on this agreement. The most important thing is to be as detailed as possible.

SHARED IN-HOME CARE

Some families pool their resources and share an in-home child care provider. These arrangements are ideal for neighbors or co-workers with children who are close in age. Just as a written agreement between a family and a child care worker can clarify expectations and prevent conflicts, written understanding between the two families who are sharing a child care provider can accomplish the same objectives. If you share in-home care with another family, be sure you both agree on the key issues before drafting your contract with the child care worker, including location of the care, performance standards, splitting expenses, termination procedures and supervision.

The following are step-by-step directions on how to fill out the child care contract. A tear-out version is provided at the end of this chapter.

Begin by providing details on the people involved and the location of the child care.

a. In the first blank, write in your name or the family name of those arranging for the child care—for example, Barbara Clark or the Clark Family. For the rest of the contract, you will be referred to as "Employer".

b. Write in the name of the person who has agreed to be the child care provider, the "Employee."

c. List all the children who are to receive care and their current ages—for example, Kelly (age 4), Jamie (age 2) and Thomas (age 1).

d. List the street address of your home. Include the city, state and zip code.

1. Beginning Date

Include the month, day and year of the first day of work.

2. Training Period

To get things off to a good start, many parents stay at home with the child care worker the first few days or weeks of employment. This gives everyone the chance to know each other and to see how the arrangement works. A training period helps your employee get to know your home and neighborhood and the exact way you want things done.

If you have a training period, please provide details here—for example: "There shall be a training period during *the first two weeks*. During this training period, *the employee will work a reduced schedule, to be arranged with the employer*.

If you do not plan to provide any training period, leave this item blank.

3. *Responsibilities*

Spell out what care is to be provided, with as much detail as possible. Our sample includes a checklist of broad categories of responsibilities. Check the boxes that apply to your situation and then add more specific information in the space provided.

Also, when your situation changes (new baby, new job), be sure to re-evaluate these responsibilities and change the contract as necessary.

a. Under Cooking and Nutrition, you might write in *"Prepare meals for and feed children daily and cook dinner for entire family two nights each week"* or *"Prepare vegetarian meals."*

b. Under Bathing and Personal Care, you could note *"Bathe each child every other day, and more frequently as needed."*

c. If your child has any particular health or medical needs, specify them under Health and Medical Care—for example, if your child has diabetes and requires regular shots, write this in—for example, *"Treat Kelly's diabetes with insulin shots according to the following daily schedule"*—then specify the schedule.

d. Under Social and Recreational, you might write in *"Arrange play dates for the children"* or *"Take children to the park every day."*

e. Under Transportation, indicate tasks such as *"Drive the children to school each morning."*

f. If your babysitter or au pair will be running regular errands or doing weekly grocery shopping, note that under Shopping and Errands—for example, *"Do grocery shopping once a week, pick up family's dry cleaning and run errands in neighborhood as requested."*

g. If one of the responsibilities is housework, provide details under Housecleaning, such as *"Keep kitchen and children's rooms clean and tidy"* or *"Clean upstairs bedrooms and bathrooms on Tuesday mornings when Kelly is at preschool."*

   If your child care worker is responsible for all your family's housecleaning, attach a separate list of housecleaning responsibilities. To prepare this list use Clause 2 of the Contract for Housekeeping Services provided in this chapter.

h. Some child care workers also wash and iron the family's clothes. Under Ironing and Laundry, specify these responsibilities, such as: *"Do laundry for children only"* or *"Do family's laundry and ironing at least twice a week."*

i. Use the category Other Responsibilities to add things such as *"Keep a daily log of times and amounts of formula baby drinks"* or *"Take care of the family cat."*

4. *Payment Terms*

Child care workers generally get paid in one of several ways and on various schedules which may include a salary review.

a. If your child care worker lives in your house, you will probably pay a flat fee per month. If your babysitter comes into your home for one or more days per week, you may pay either an hourly wage, generally ranging from $5 to $10 per hour, or a flat salary. How much you pay depends on many factors:

   - the number and ages of your children—for example, infant care is more expensive than babysitting a school-age child
   - the type of care provided and responsibilities
   - the number of hours, time of day and regularity of the schedule
   - the experience and training of the employee
   - benefits such as room and board, and
   - the going rate in your community. You can get this by asking around or checking want ads for child care.

   Check off the deductions you will take from the child care worker's paycheck, including Social Security and and state and federal income taxes. (See Section C above for guidance on these deductions.) If you will deduct the costs of any lo-

long-distance phone calls your babysitter or au pair makes, check off this item. If there are any other deductions, such as the cost of insurance premiums, specify them under "Other deductions."

b. Here you can specify whether and when a regular salary review will occur—for example, *"Salary will be reviewed after the first six months of employment, and annually thereafter."*

c. Specify the interval and dates on which you pay for care—for example, if the payment is weekly, specify the day; if payment is twice each month, specify the dates, such as the 15th and the 30th, or the last previous weekday if either date falls on a weekend.

5. *Hours of Care*

Child care is usually provided during set times, such as 8 A.M. to 6 P.M. weekdays or noon to 4 P.M. on Tuesdays and Thursdays. There may be an open-ended agreement with live-in help, but be careful on this. No matter how great you and your family are, no one wants to be on call 24 hours a day.

Be sure to provide information on when and how additional hours may be required and include the pay rate for such arrangements—for example, *"Additional hours of child care are subject to Employee's approval and will be paid at the rate of $8.00 per hour or $100 per 24-hour period when the Employee accompanies the children on vacation."*

6. *Benefits*

There are a range of benefits you may give your employee, in addition to those that are legally required (see Section C, above):

a. Meals

If you want to limit the amount of money you'll spend on your employee's meals, particularly if he or she is doing the grocery shopping and wants filet mignon every night, specify that here.

b. Room and board

c. Sick leave—for example, *"Five paid sick days a year."*

d. Vacation days

Be sure to specify how vacation time accrues and when it must be used—for example *"One week paid vacation after each 6-month period of work with choice of vacation days subject to Employer approval; all vacation must be used during the year in which it accumulates."*

e. Holidays

You may want to specify the paid holidays—for example: Christmas, New Year's, 4th of July, Labor Day and Thanksgiving.

f. Health insurance

Indicate the details of any coverage—for example, *"Full health insurance under family's group medical plan after a year of employment"* or *"Annual lump sum payment of $500 to be made to health insurance company of Employee's choice."*

g. Transportation, such as *"Reimbursement, up to $15 per week, for taking bus to work"*

h. Other—for example, *"Personal use of family car"* (note any restrictions) or *"A private telephone line and monthly service charges, excluding costs of toll and long-distance phone calls."*

7. *Termination Policy*

You want to be able to fire your employee immediately, at any time for any cause. You don't want to guarantee a year's employment to someone who doesn't work out after a few weeks—who turns out to be incompetent, who the kids don't like, who violates your house policy of no smoking—whatever the reason.

This clause also allows your employee to quit at any time, rather than remain in a position where he or she is badly treated, where working conditions are intolerable or where promises regarding pay and benefits are not kept.

8. *Probation*

You and your employee should agree on a review or probationary period—for example, two or four weeks—after which you can both evaluate the situation and how it compares to your expectations.

You want to provide an incentive for good employees to stay a long time and give you adequate notice—as much as possible, but a minimum of two weeks—when they do leave. One suggestion is to provide severance pay for employees who give notice and continue doing a competent job until they leave. The amount of the severance pay could increase the longer the employee has worked.

You might provide one-week of severance pay after an initial probationary period, two weeks of severance pay after one year and three weeks after two years. An employee who left after two years of service might get three weeks of severance pay regardless of whether you fired her or she quit, as long as she provided the required amount of notice.

9. *Additional Agreements And Amendments*

You might add here additional understandings that you and the employee have reached—for example, *"Employer and Employee additionally agree that employee will take a Red Cross course on CPR for children and infants within the first month of employment. Employer will pay for the course and compensate the employee for her time taking the course."*

Other additional agreements include *"No smoking in house," "No television-watching for children except Sesame Street;" "No spanking or physical discipline"* or *"No overnight guests."*

This is also the place to address any special circumstances—for example, if your au pair wants to take a part-time night job outside of your home during "off-duty" time, and you want to specify the conditions for this type of arrangement.

If you wish to add additional clauses to this contract, perhaps Clause 2 on housecleaning responsibilities from the second contract in this chapter, take the following steps:

- Label a blank 8 1/2" by 11" piece of paper "Attachment A".
- Reproduce on Attachment A the clause or clauses you wish to use in this contract, and fill them in.
- Use the following language in this clause to make Attachment A part of this contract: *"Employer and Employee incorporate the clauses set out on Attachment A as if fully set out herein."*
- Sign or initial (both you and the employee) each clause on Attachment A.

The last part of this clause—"All agreements relating to child care under this contract are incorporated in this contract. Any modification to the contract must be in writing."—is fairly standard in written contracts. First, it expressly says that the contract covers your entire agreement about child care. Second, it provides that any changes to the contract must be in writing. Together, these provisions prevent you or your employee from later claiming that additional oral or written promises were made, but just not included in the written agreement.

10. *Place of Execution*

In this clause—"This agreement is executed by Employer and Employee at _Berkeley, California_ on _September 1, 199—_"—you specify where (city and state) and when you sign the contract. "Executed" is simply a legal term meaning by signing the piece of paper, both sides are acknowledging that it contains the agreement they have reached. If there's any legal problem with the contract later—for example, a dispute over the hours or type of work to be performed—it will likely be resolved by the courts where it was executed.

EMERGENCY PROCEDURES AND HOUSE RULES

While not necessarily part of an employment contract or agreement, it's also a good idea to prepare a written set of house rules and emergency procedures, for example:

- Emergency contacts, including parents' work address and phone numbers, friends' and relatives' names and numbers, and phone numbers for pediatrician and hospital, poison control center, the police and fire departments, and a local taxi company
- Information on children's health care, such as any allergies
- Written permission for your employee to arrange medical treatment your children may need in the case of an emergency. Ask your pediatrician or local emergency room for a standard permission form
- Directions for using appliances and electronic equipment such as the VCR
- Earthquake and tornado procedures (depending on where you live)

2. Housekeeping Services

If you employ a part-time housekeeper who cleans your house one or more days each week or a full-time housekeeper who comes in every day or lives in your home, use the following form.

Your written agreement should clearly specify the housecleaner's responsibilities, hours, benefits, amount and schedule of payment and termination policy. The step-by-step instructions below should help you complete the housekeeping contract. A tear-out version is provided at the end of this chapter.

Begin by providing details on the people involved and the location of the housecleaning.

a. In the first blank, write in your name or the family name of those arranging for the housecleaning—for example, Sandy Lewis or the Lewis Family. For the rest of the contract you will be referred to as "Employer."

b. Write in the name of the person who has agreed to clean your house, the "Employee".

c. List the street address of your home. Include the city, state and zip code.

1. Beginning Date

Include the month, day and year of the first day of work.

2. Housecleaning Responsibilities

Spell out what housecleaning and other domestic work is to be done with as much detail as possible.

The sample contract includes a checklist of rooms to be cleaned, with space to add more specific information. For example, next to Living Room, you might put *"Clean out fireplace every three months."* For Dining Room, you might note *"Wet mop floors only,"* or for Kitchen, *"Wax floor once each week."* Under Special Instructions, you could put *"Wash inside all windows twice a month"* or *"Dust mini-blinds at least once a month."*

The checklist of responsibilities also includes any work to be done outside the house; one example might be *"Clean the rails of the deck,"* or *"Sweep the front porch."*

3. *Other Responsibilities*

Here you list other non-cleaning types of work you want your employee to do, such as ironing and laundry or organizing your kitchen cupboards.

4. *Supplies and Equipment*

Most housecleaners will use your cleaning supplies, vacuum cleaner and other equipment—although many will specify the brands or types of products they prefer to use. Generally, you are responsible for purchasing all supplies and keeping them in stock, but here you would note any exceptions. A housekeeper who brings in most of his or her own equipment and cleaning supplies might be considered an independent contractor (see Chapter 6, Section 7).

5. *Payment Terms*

Housecleaners generally get paid in one of several ways and on various schedules.

a. If your housekeeper lives out, you would probably pay either an hourly wage ($8 to $15 per hour) or a flat salary. If a housekeeper lives in your home, you would usually pay a flat monthly fee.

   How much you pay depends on many factors:

   - the type of housecleaning and other responsibilities
   - the number of hours, days and regularity of the schedule
   - the experience and training of the employee
   - the going rate in your community. You can ask around and check local want ads for comparable rates.

   Check off the deductions you will take from the employee's paycheck, including Social Security and and state and federal income taxes. (See Section C above for guidance on these deductions.) If you will deduct the costs of any local or long-distance phone calls your employee makes, check this item. If there are any other deductions, such as payments for insurance premiums, specify them under "Other deductions."

b. Here you specify the interval and dates on which you pay for care—for example, if the payment is weekly, specify the day of the week; if the payment is twice each month, specify the dates, such as the 15th and the 30th, or the last previous weekday if either date falls on a weekend.

6. *Hours*

Specify the days and times, such as daily from 8:30 A.M. to 3:30 P.M. or Monday through Saturday from 10 A.M. to 2 P.M.

Be sure to provide information on when and how additional hours may be required and include the pay rate for such arrangements—for example, "Additional hours of work are subject to Employee's approval and will be paid at the rate of $ *10.00* per hour."

7. *Benefits*

There are a range of benefits you may give your employee, in addition to those that are legally required (see Section C, above):

a. Lunch or other meals

b. Room and board for live-in help

c. Sick leave—for example—*"Five paid sick days a year"*

d. Vacation days

   Be sure to specify how vacation time accrues and when it must be used—for example *"One week paid vacation after each 6-month period of work with choice of vacation days subject to Employer's approval; all vacation must be used during the year in which it accumulates."*

e. Holidays

   You may want to specify the paid holidays—for example, Christmas, New Year's, 4th of July, Labor Day and Thanksgiving.

f. Health insurance

Indicate the details of any coverage—for example, *"Full health insurance under family's group medical plan after a year of employment"* or *"Annual lump sum payment of $500 to be made to health insurance company of Employee's choice."*

g. Transportation, such as *"Reimbursement, up to $15 per week, for taking bus to work"*

h. Other—for example, *"Personal use of family car"* (note any restrictions).

8. Termination Policy

You want to be able to fire your employee immediately, at any time for any cause. You don't want to guarantee a year's employment to someone who doesn't work out after a few weeks—who turns out to be incompetent or is very careless, who violates your house policy of no smoking—whatever the reason.

This clause also allows your employee to quit at any time, rather than remain in a position where he or she is badly treated, where working conditions are intolerable or where promises regarding pay and benefits are not kept.

9. Additional Agreements and Amendments

You might add here additional requirements—for example, *"No smoking in house,"* or *"No guests."*

If you wish to add additional clauses to this contract, take the following steps:

- Label a blank 8 1/2" by 11" piece of paper "Attachment A".
- Reproduce on Attachment A the clause or clauses you wish to use in this contract, and fill them in.
- Use the following language in this clause to make Attachment A part of this contract: *"Employer and Employee incorporate the clauses set out on Attachment A as if fully set out herein."*
- Sign or initial (both you and the employee) each clause on Attachment A.

The last part of this clause—"All agreements relating to housekeeping services under this contract are incorporated in this contract. Any modification to the contract must be in writing." —is fairly standard in written contracts. First, it expressly says that the contract covers your entire agreement. Second, it provides that any changes to the contract must be in writing. Together, these provisions prevent you or your employee from later claiming that additional oral or written promises were made, but just not included in the written agreement.

10. Place of Execution

In this clause—"This agreement is executed by Employer and Employee at *Berkeley, California* on *September 1, 199—* "—you specify where (city and state) and when you sign the contract. "Executed" is simply a legal term meaning by signing the piece of paper, both sides are acknowledging that it contains the agreement they have reached. If there's any legal problem with the contract later—for example, a dispute over the hours or type of work to be performed—it will likely be resolved by the courts where it was executed.

CONTRACT FOR CHILD CARE

____, Employer, contracts with ____, Employee, to provide child care for ____, Children, at ____ ____.

1. Beginning Date

Employment shall begin on ____________________, 19____.

2. Training Period

There shall be a training period during the first ____________ of employment. During this training period, ____

3. Responsibilities

The care to be provided under this agreement consists of the following responsibilities (check the appropriate boxes and provide details):

☐ a. Cooking and Nutrition ____

☐ b. Bathing and Personal Care ____

☐ c. Health and Medical Care ____

☐ d. Social and Recreational ____

☐ e. Transportation ____

☐ f. Shopping and Errands ____

☐ g. Housecleaning ____

☐ h. Ironing and Laundry ____

☐ i. Other Responsibilities ____________________

____

4. Payment Terms

a. The Employee will be paid as follows:

☐ $ __________ per hour

☐ $ __________ per month

☐ $ __________ Other ____________________

with the following deductions and exceptions:

☐ Social Security ____________________

☐ Federal income taxes ____________________

☐ State income taxes ____________________

☐ Local and long-distance phone charges ____________________

☐ Other deductions ____________________

b. A salary review will occur ____________________.

c. The Employee shall be paid on the specified intervals and dates:

☐ Once a week on every ____________________.

☐ Twice a month on ____________________.

☐ Once a month on ____________________.

5. Hours of Care

Hours of child care will be ____________________.

Additional hours of child care are subject to Employee's approval and will be paid at the rate of $ __________ per hour or

____________________.

6. Benefits

Employer will provide Employee with the following benefits:

☐ a. Meals ____________________

____

☐ b. Room and Board ____________________

____

☐ c. Sick Leave ____________________

____

☐ d. Vacation Days ____

____

☐ e. Holidays ____

____

☐ f. Health Insurance ____

____

☐ g. Transportation ____

____

☐ h. Other ____

____

7. Termination Policy

Either Employee or Employer may terminate this agreement at any time, for any reason, without notice.

8. Probation

After an initial probationary period of ____________________, Employee is entitled to severance pay as follows: __________

____

provided that at least ______________________________ notice is provided and Employee provides satisfactory child care during the notice period.

9. Additional Agreements and Amendments

a. Employer and Employee additionally agree that: ____

____

b. All agreements relating to child care under this contract are incorporated in this contract. Any modification to the contract must be in writing.

10. Place of Execution

This agreement is executed by Employer and Employee at ______________________________

______________________________, on ______________________________.

Employer's Signature	Employee's Signature
Address	Address
______________________________	______________________________
______________________________	______________________________

MAKE TWO COPIES OF THIS AGREEMENT, ONE FOR EACH PARTY.

CONTRACT FOR HOUSEKEEPING SERVICES

______________________________, Employer, agrees to contract with

______________________________, Employee, to work at

______________________________.

1. Beginning Date

Employment shall begin on ______________________, 19______.

2. Housecleaning Responsibilities

The responsibilities to be provided under this agreement consist of cleaning the following rooms and areas:

☐ Interior: ______________________________

☐ Living room: ______________________________

☐ Dining room: ______________________________

☐ Kitchen: ______________________________

☐ Bedrooms: ______________________________

☐ Bathrooms: ______________________________

☐ Family room: ______________________________

☐ Study or den: ______________________________

☐ Basement: ______________________________

☐ Laundry room: ______________________________

☐ Hallways and Entryways: ______________________________

☐ Staircases: ______________________________

☐ Other Rooms or Interior Areas: ______________________________

SPECIAL INSTRUCTIONS: ______________________________

____

____

____

☐ Exterior: ______________________________

☐ Front porch or deck: ______________________________

☐ Back porch or deck: ______________________________

☐ Garage: ______________________________

☐ Pool, hot tub or sauna: ______________________________

☐ Other exterior areas: ______________________________

SPECIAL INSTRUCTIONS: ____________________

____

____

____

3. Other Responsibilities

Employee also agrees to do the following non-cleaning types of work:

☐ Cooking: ____________________

☐ Laundry: ____________________

☐ Ironing: ____________________

☐ Shopping and errands: ____________________

☐ Gardening: ____________________

☐ Other: ____________________

4. Supplies and Equipment

Employer will provide all housecleaning supplies, vacuum cleaner and other equipment, except ____________________

____

5. Payment Terms

a. Employee will be paid as follows:

☐ $ __________ per hour

☐ $ __________ per month

☐ $ __________ Other ____________________

with the following deductions and exceptions:

☐ Social Security ____________________

☐ Federal income taxes ____________________

☐ State income taxes ____________________

☐ Local and long-distance phone charges ____________________

☐ Other deductions ____________________

____

b. Employee shall be paid on the specified intervals and dates:

☐ Once a week on every ____________________.

☐ Twice a month on ____________________.

☐ Once a month on ____________________.

6. Hours

Dates and hours of housekeeping will be: ____________________.

Additional hours of work are subject to Employee's approval and will be paid at the rate of $ ____________ per hour or

____________________.

7. Benefits

Employer will provide Housekeeper with the following benefits:

a. ☐ Meals ____________________

b. ☐ Room and Board ____________________

c. ☐ Sick Leave ____________________

d. ☐ Vacation Days ____________________

e. ☐ Holidays ____________________

f. ☐ Health Insurance ____________________

g. ☐ Transportation ____________________

h. ☐ Other ____________________

8. Termination Policy

Either Employer or Employee can terminate this agreement at any time, for any reason, without notice, with the following exceptions:

____

9. Additional Agreements and Amendments

Employer and Employee additionally agree that: ____________________.

____

All agreements relating to the work under this contract are incorporated in this contract. Any modification to the contract shall be in writing.

10. Place of Execution

This agreement is executed by Employer and Employee at ______________________________

______________________________, on ______________________________.

______________________________	______________________________
Employer's Signature	Employee's Signature
______________________________	______________________________
Address	Address
______________________________	______________________________
______________________________	______________________________

MAKE TWO COPIES OF THIS AGREEMENT, ONE FOR EACH PARTY.

Appendix

STATE CONSUMER PROTECTION OFFICES

State	Phone Number	Address
Alabama	(205) 242-7334 (800) 392-5658	Consumer Protection Division, Office of Attorney General, 11 South Union St., Montgomery, AL 36130
Arkansas	(501) 682-2007 (800) 482-8982	Advocacy Division of Attorney General's Office, 200 Tower Bldg., 323 Center St., Little Rock, AR 72201
California	(916) 445-1254 (800) 344-9940	Department of Consumer Affairs, Consumer Assistance Office, 1020 N St., Rm. 501, Sacramento, CA 95814
Colorado	(303) 620-4581 (800) 332-2071	Consumer Protection Unit, Office of Attorney General, 110 16th St., 10th Fl., Denver, CO 80202
Connecticut	(203) 566-4999 (800) 842-2649	Commissioner Mary Heslin, Department of Consumer Protection, State Office Bldg., 165 Capitol Ave., Hartford, CT 06106
Delaware	(302) 577-3250	Division of Consumer Affairs, 820 North French St., Delaware State Office Bldg., 4th Fl., Wilmington, DE 19801
District of Columbia	(202) 727-7076	Department of Consumer and Regulatory Affairs, 614 H St., NW, Rm. 106, Washington, DC 20001
Florida	(904) 488-2226 (800) 327-3382	Division of Consumer Services, Dept. of Agriculture and Consumer Services, 218 Mayo Bldg., Tallahassee, FL 32399
Georgia	(404) 651-8600 (800) 869-1123	Office of Consumer Affairs, 2 Martin Luther King Jr. Drive, Plaza Level Tower, Atlanta, GA 30334
Hawaii	(808) 548-2560	Office of Consumer Protection, Dept. of Commerce and Consumer Affairs, 828 Fort Street Mall, Rm. 600B, Honolulu, HI 96813
Idaho	(208) 334-2400 (800) 432-3545	Business Regulation Division, Office of Attorney General, Statehouse, Boise, ID 83720
Illinois	(217) 782-9011 (800) 252-8666	Consumer Protection Division, Office of Attorney General, 500 South 2nd St., Springfield, IL 62706
Indiana	(317) 232-6330 (800) 383-5516	Consumer Protection Division, Office of Attorney General, 219 State House, Indianapolis, IN 46204

State	Phone Number	Address
Iowa	(515) 281-5926	Consumer Protection Division, Office of Attorney General, 1300 East Walnut, 2nd Fl., Des Moines, IA 50319
Kansas	(913) 296-3751 (800) 432-2310	Consumer Protection Division, Office of Attorney General, Judicial Center, Topeka, KS 66612
Kentucky	(502) 564-2200 (800) 432-9257	Consumer Protection Division, Office of Attorney General, 209 St. Clair St., Frankfort, KY 40601
Louisiana	(504) 342-7013	Consumer Protection Section, Office of Attorney General, P.O. Box 94005, Baton Rouge, LA 70804-9005
Maine	(207) 582-8718 (800) 332-8529	Bureau of Consumer Credit Protection, State House, Station No. 35, Augusta, ME 04333-0035
Maryland	(301) 528-8662 (800) 969-5766	Consumer Protection Division, Office of Attorney General, 200 St. Paul Pl., Baltimore, MD 21202-2022
Massachusetts	(617) 727-7780	Consumer Protection Division, Dept. of Attorney General, 131 Tremont St., Boston, MA 02111
Michigan	(517) 373-0947	Consumers Council, 414 Hollister Bldg., 106 West Allegan St., Lansing, MI 48933
Minnesota	(612) 296-2331	Office of Consumer Services, Office of Attorney General, 117 University Ave., Rm. 124, St. Paul, MN 55155
Mississippi	(601) 354-6018	Consumer Protection Division, Office of Attorney General, P.O. Box 22947, Jackson, MS 39225
Missouri	(314) 751-3321 (800) 392-8222	Consumer Protection Division, Office of Attorney General, P.O. Box 899, Jefferson City, MO 65102
Montana	(406) 444-4312	Consumer Affairs Unit, Dept. of Commerce, 1424 9th Ave., Helena, MT 59620
Nebraska	(402) 471-4723	Consumer Protection Division, Dept. of Justice, 2115 State Capitol, P.O. Box 98920, Lincoln, NB 68509
Nevada	(702) 486-7355	Consumer Affairs Division, Dept. of Consumer Affairs, State Mail Room Complex, Las Vegas, NV 89158
New Hampshire	(603) 271-3641	Consumer Protection and Antitrust Division, Office of Attorney General, State House Annex, Concord, NH 03301
New Jersey	(201) 648-4010	Office of Consumer Protection, 1100 Raymond Blvd., Newark, NJ 07102
New Mexico	(505) 827-6910 (800) 432-2070	Consumer and Economic Crime Division, Office of Attorney General, P.O. Drawer 1508, Santa Fe, NM 87504
New York	(518) 474-8583	Consumer Protection Board, 99 Washington Ave., Albany, NY 12210
North Carolina	(919) 733-7741	Consumer Protection Section, Office of Attorney General, Dept. of Justice, P.O. Box 629, Raleigh, NC 27602
North Dakota	(701) 224-3404 (800) 472-2600	Consumer Fraud Division, Office of Attorney General, 600 East Blvd., Bismark, ND 58505
Ohio	(614) 466-4986 (800) 282-0515	Consumer Protection Division, Office of Attorney General, 30 East Broad St, 25th Fl., Columbus, OH 43266-0410
Oklahoma	(405) 521-3921	Consumer Affairs Division, Office of Attorney General, 112 State Capitol Bldg., Oklahoma City, OK 73105
Oregon	(503) 378-4320	Financial Fraud Section, Dept. of Justice, Justice Bldg., Salem, OR 97310

State	Phone Number	Address
Pennsylvania	(717) 787-9707 (800) 441-2555	Bureau of Consumer Protection, Office of Attorney General, Strawberry Sq., 14th Fl., Harrisburg, PA 17120
Rhode Island	(401) 277-2104 (800) 852-7776	Consumer Protection Division, Dept. of Attorney General, 72 Pine St., Providence, RI 02903
South Carolina	(803) 734-9452 (800) 922-1594	Dept. of Consumer Affairs, P.O. Box 5757, Columbia, SC 29250
South Dakota	(605) 773-4400	Division of Consumer Affairs, Office of Attorney General, State Capitol Bldg., Pierre, SD 57501
Tennessee	(615) 741-4737 (800) 342-8385	Division of Consumer Affairs, Dept. of Commerce and Insurance, 500 James Robertson Pkwy., 5th Fl., Nashville, TN 37243-0600
Texas	(512) 463-2070	Consumer Protection Division, Office of Attorney General, P.O. Box 12548, Capitol Station, Austin, TX 78711
Utah	(801) 530-6601	Division of Consumer Protection, Dept. of Business Regulation, 160 East 3rd South, P.O. Box 45802, Salt Lake City, UT 84145-0802
Vermont	(802) 656-3183	Consumer Assistance, Office of Attorney General, Terrill Hall—University of Vermont, Burlington, VT 05405
Virginia	(804) 786-2042	Office of Consumer Affairs, Dept. of Agriculture and Consumer Services, Rm. 101, Washington Bldg., 1100 Bank St., Richmond, VA 23219
Washington	(206) 464-7744 (800) 551-4636	Consumer and Business Fair Practices Division, Office of Attorney General, 900 4th Ave., Rm. 2000, Seattle, WA 98164
West Virginia	(304) 348-8986 (800) 368-8808	Consumer Protection Division, Office of Attorney General, 812 Quarrier St., 6th Fl., Charleston, WV 25301
Wisconsin	(608) 266-9836 (800) 422-7128	Division of Trade and Consumer Protection, Dept. of Agriculture, Trade and Consumer Protection, 801 West Badger Rd., P.O. Box 8911, Madison, WI 53708
Wyoming	(307) 777-7841	Consumer Affairs Division, Office of Attorney General, 123 State Capitol Bldg., Cheyenne, WY 82002

LIST OF CONTRACTS

nolo CATALOG

ESTATE PLANNING & PROBATE

Plan Your Estate With a Living Trust
Attorney Denis Clifford
National 1st Edition
This book covers every significant aspect of estate planning and gives detailed specific, instructions for preparing a living trust, a document that lets your family avoid expensive and lengthy probate court proceedings after your death. *Plan Your Estate* includes all the tear-out forms and step-by-step instructions to let you prepare an estate plan designed for your special needs.
$19.95/NEST

Nolo's Simple Will Book
Attorney Denis Clifford
National 2nd Edition
It's easy to write a legally valid will using this book. The instructions and forms enable people to draft a will for all needs, including naming a personal guardian for minor children, leaving property to minor children or young adults and updating a will when necessary. Good in all states except Louisiana.
$17.95/SWIL

The Power of Attorney Book
Attorney Denis Clifford
National 4th Edition
Who will take care of your affairs, and make your financial and medical decisions if you can't? With this book you can appoint someone you trust to carry out your wishes and stipulate exactly what kind of care you want or don't want. Includes Durable Power of Attorney and Living Will Forms.
$19.95/POA

How to Probate an Estate
Julia Nissley
California 5th Edition
If you find yourself responsible for winding up the legal and financial affairs of a deceased family member or friend, you can often save costly attorneys' fees by handling the probate process yourself. This book shows you the simple procedures you can use to transfer assets that don't require probate, including property held in joint tenancy or living trusts or as community property.
$34.95/PAE

The Conservatorship Book
Lisa Goldoftas & Attorney Carolyn Farren
California 1st Edition
When a family member or close relative becomes incapacitated due to illness or age, it may be necessary to name a conservator for taking charge of their medical and financial affairs. *The Conservatorship Book* will help you determine when and what kind of conservatorship is necessary. The book comes with complete instructions and all the forms necessary to file conservatorship documents, appear in court, be appointed conservator and end a conservatorship when it is no longer necessary.
$24.95/CON

LEGAL REFORM

Legal Breakdown: 40 Ways to Fix Our Legal System
Nolo Press Editors and Staff
National 1st Edition
Legal Breakdown presents 40 common sense proposals to make our legal system fairer, faster, cheaper and more accessible. It explains such things as why we should abolish probate, take divorce out of court, treat jurors better and give them more power, and make a host of other fundamental changes.
$8.95/LEG

GOING TO COURT

Everybody's Guide to Small Claims Court
Attorney Ralph Warner
National 5th Edition
California 9th Edition
These books will help you decide if you should sue in small claims court, show you how to file and serve papers, tell you what to bring to court and how to collect a judgment.
National $15.95/NSCC
California $14.95/ CSCC

Fight Your Ticket
Attorney David Brown
California 4th Edition
This book shows you how to fight an unfair traffic ticket—when you're stopped, at arraignment, at trial and on appeal.
$17.95/FYT

Collect Your Court Judgment
Gini Graham Scott, Attorney Stephen Elias & Lisa Goldoftas
California 2nd Edition
This book contains step-by-step instructions and all the forms you need to collect a court judgment from the debtor's bank accounts, wages, business receipts, real estate or other assets.
$19.95/JUDG

How to Change Your Name
Attorneys David Loeb & David Brown
California 5th Edition
This book explains how to change your name legally and provides all the necessary court forms with detailed instructions on how to fill them out.
$19.95/NAME

The Criminal Records Book
Attorney Warren Siegel
California 3rd Edition
This book shows you step-by-step how to seal criminal records, dismiss convictions, destroy marijuana records and reduce felony convictions.
$19.95/CRIM

MONEY MATTERS

Barbara Kaufman's Consumer Action Guide

Barbara Kaufman
California 1st Edition
This practical handbook is filled with information on hundreds of consumer topics. Barbara Kaufman, the Bay Area's award-winning host and producer of KCBS Radio's *Call for Action*, gives consumers access to their legal rights, providing addresses and phone numbers of where to complain where things to wrong, and providing resources if more help is necessary.
$14.95/CAG

Money Troubles: Legal Strategies to Cope With Your Debts

Attorney Robin Leonard
National 1st Edition
Are you behind on your credit card bills or loan payments? If you are, then *Money Troubles* is exactly what you need. Covering everything from knowing what your rights are—and asserting them to helping you evaluate your individual situation, this practical, straightforward book is for anyone who needs help understanding and dealing with the complex and often scary topic of debts.
$16.95/MT

How to File for Bankruptcy

Attorneys Stephen Elias, Albin Renauer & Robin Leonard
National 3rd Edition
Trying to decide whether or not filing for bankruptcy makes sense? *How to File for Bankruptcy* contains an overview of the process and all the forms plus step-by-step instructions on the procedures to follow.
$24.95/HFB

Simple Contracts for Personal Use

Attorney Stephen Elias & Marcia Stewart
National 2nd Edition
This book contains clearly written legal form contracts to buy and sell property, borrow and lend money, store and lend personal property, release others from personal liability, or pay a contractor to do home repairs. Includes agreements to arrange child care and contract with caterers, photographers and other service providers for special events.
$16.95/CONT

FAMILY MATTERS

The Living Together Kit

Attorneys Toni Ihara & Ralph Warner
National 6th Edition
The Living Together Kit is a detailed guide designed to help the increasing number of unmarried couples living together understand the laws that affect them. Sample agreements and instructions are included.
$17.95/LTK

A Legal Guide for Lesbian and Gay Couples

Attorneys Hayden Curry & Denis Clifford
National 6th Edition
Laws designed to regulate and protect unmarried couples don't apply to lesbian and gay couples. This book shows you step-by-step how to write a living-together contract, plan for medical emergencies, and plan your estates. Includes forms, sample agreements and lists of both national lesbian and gay legal organizations, and AIDS organizations.
$17.95/LG

The Guardianship Book

Lisa Goldoftas & Attorney David Brown
California 1st Edition
The Guardianship Book provides step-by-step instructions and the forms needed to obtain a legal guardianship without a lawyer.
$19.95/GB

How to Do Your Own Divorce

Attorney Charles Sherman
(Texas Ed. by Sherman & Simons)
California 17th Edition & Texas 2nd Edition
These books contain all the forms and instructions you need to do your divorce without a lawyer.
California $18.95/CDIV
Texas $14.95/TDIV

Practical Divorce Solutions

Attorney Charles Sherman
California 2nd Edition
This book is a valuable guide to the emotional aspects of divorce as well as an overview of the legal and financial decisions that must be made.
$12.95/PDS

California Marriage & Divorce Law

Attorneys Ralph Warner, Toni Ihara & Stephen Elias
California 11th Edition
This book explains community property, pre-nuptial contracts, foreign marriages, buying a house, getting a divorce, dividing property, and more.
$19.95/MARR

How to Adopt Your Stepchild in California

Frank Zagone & Attorney Mary Randolph
California 3rd Edition
There are many emotional, financial and legal reasons to adopt a stepchild, but among the most pressing legal reasons is the need to avoid confusion over inheritance or guardianship. This book provides sample forms and step-by-step instructions for completing a simple uncontested adoption by a stepparent
$19.95/ADOP

BUSINESS

How to Write a Business Plan
Mike McKeever
National 3rd Edition
If you're thinking of starting a business or raising money to expand an existing one, this book will show you how to write the business plan and loan package necessary to finance your business and make it work.
$17.95/SBS

Marketing Without Advertising
Michael Phillips & Salli Rasberry
National 1st Edition
This book outlines practical steps for building and expanding a small business without spending a lot of money on advertising.
$14.00/MWA

The Partnership Book
Attorneys Denis Clifford & Ralph Warner
National 4th Edition
This book shows you step-by-step how to write a solid partnership agreement that meets your needs. It covers initial contributions to the business, wages, profit-sharing, buy-outs, death or retirement of a partner and disputes.
$24.95/PART

How to Form Your Own Nonprofit Corporation
Attorney Anthony Mancuso
National 1st Edition
This book explains the legal formalities involved and provides detailed information on the differences in the law among 50 states. It also contains forms for the Articles, Bylaws and Minutes you need, along with complete instructions for obtaining federal 501 (c) (3) tax exemptions and qualifying for public charity status.
$24.95/NNP

The California Nonprofit Corporation Handbook
Attorney Anthony Mancuso
California 6th Edition
This book shows you step-by-step how to form and operate a nonprofit corporation in California. It includes the latest corporate and tax law changes, and the forms for the Articles, Bylaws and Minutes.
$29.95/NON

How to Form Your Own Corporation
Attorney Anthony Mancuso
California 7th Edition
New York 2nd Edition
Florida 3rd Edition
These books contain the forms, instructions and tax information you need to incorporate a small business yourself and save hundreds of dollars in lawyers' fees.
California $29.95/CCOR
New York $24.95/NYCO
Florida $24.95/FLCO

The California Professional Corporation Handbook
Attorney Anthony Mancuso
California 4th Edition
Health care professionals, lawyers, accountants and members of certain other professions must fulfill special requirements when forming a corporation in California. This book contains up-to-date tax information plus all the forms and instructions necessary to form a California professional corporation.
$34.95/PROF

The Independent Paralegal's Handbook
Attorney Ralph Warner
National 2nd Edition
The Independent Paralegal's Handbook provides legal and business guidelines for those who want to take routine legal work out of the law office and offer it for a reasonable fee in an independent business.
$19.95/ PARA

Getting Started as an Independent Paralegal
(Two Audio Tapes)
Attorney Ralph Warner
National 1st Edition
Approximately three hours in all, these tapes are a carefully edited version of a seminar given by Nolo Press founder Ralph Warner. They are designed to be used with *The Independent Paralegal's Handbook.*
$24.95/GSIP

PATENT, COPYRIGHT & TRADEMARK

Patent It Yourself
Attorney David Pressman
National 3rd Edition
From the patent search to the actual application, this book covers everything from use and licensing, successful marketing and how to deal with infringement.
$34.95/PAT

The Inventor's Notebook
Fred Grissom & Attorney David Pressman
National 1st Edition
This book helps you document the process of successful independent inventing by providing forms, instructions, references to relevant areas of patent law, a bibliography of legal and non-legal aids and more.
$19.95/INOT

How to Copyright Software
Attorney M.J. Salone
National 3rd Edition
This book tells you how to register your copyright for maximum protection and discusses who owns a copyright on software developed by more than one person.
$39.95/COPY

THE NEIGHBORHOOD

Neighbor Law: Fences, Trees, Boundaries & Noise

Attorney Cora Jordan
National 1st Edition
Neighbor Law answers common questions about the subjects that most often trigger disputes between neighbors: trees, fences, boundaries and noise. It explains how to find the law and resolve disputes without a nasty lawsuit.
$14.95/NEI

Dog Law

Attorney Mary Randolph
National 1st Edition
Dog Law is a practical guide to the laws that affect dog owners and their neighbors. You'll find answers to common questions on such topics as biting, barking, veterinarians and more.
$12.95/DOG

HOMEOWNERS

How to Buy a House in California

Attorney Ralph Warner, Ira Serkes & George Devine
California 1st Edition
This book shows you how to find a house, work with a real estate agent, make an offer and negotiate intelligently. Includes information on all types of mortgages as well as private financing options.
$18.95/BHC

For Sale By Owner

George Devine
California 1st Edition
For Sale By Owner provides essential information about pricing your house, marketing it, writing a contract and going through escrow.
$24.95/FSBO

The Deeds Book

Attorney Mary Randolph
California 1st Edition
If you own real estate, you'll need to sign a new deed when you transfer the property or put it in trust as part of your estate planning. This book shows you how to find the right kind of deed, complete the tear-out forms and record them in the county recorder's public records.
$15.95/DEED

Homestead Your House

Attorneys Ralph Warner, Charles Sherman & Toni Ihara
California 8th Edition
This book shows you how to file a Declaration of Homestead and includes complete instructions and tear-out forms.
$9.95/HOME

LANDLORDS & TENANTS

The Landlord's Law Book: Vol. 1, Rights & Responsibilities

Attorneys David Brown & Ralph Warner
California 3rd Edition
This book contains information on deposits, leases and rental agreements, inspections (tenant's privacy rights), habitability (rent withholding), ending a tenancy, liability and rent control.
$29.95/LBRT

The Landlord's Law Book: Vol. 2, Evictions

Attorney David Brown
California 3rd Edition
Updated for 1991, this book will show you step-by-step how to go to court and get an eviction for a tenant who won't pay rent—and won't leave. Contains all the tear-out forms and necessary instructions.
$29.95/LBEV

Tenant's Rights

Attorneys Myron Moskovitz & Ralph Warner
California 11th Edition
This book explains the best way to handle your relationship both your landlord and your legal rights when you find yourself in disagreement. A special section on rent control cities is included.
$15.95/CTEN

OLDER AMERICANS

Elder Care: Choosing & Financing Long-Term Care

Attorney Joseph Matthews
National 1st Edition
This book will guide you in choosing and paying for long-term care, alerting you to practical concerns and explaining laws that may affect your decisions.
$16.95/ELD

Social Security, Medicare & Pensions

Attorney Joseph Matthews with Dorothy Matthews Berman
National 5th Edition
This book contains invaluable guidance through the current maze of rights and benefits for those 55 and over, including Medicare, Medicaid and Social Security retirement and disability benefits and age discrimination protections.
$15.95/SOA

JUST FOR FUN

29 Reasons Not to Go to Law School

Attorneys Ralph Warner & Toni Ihara
National 3rd Edition
Filled with humor and piercing observations, this book can save you three years, $70,000 and your sanity.
$9.95/29R

Devil's Advocates: The Unnatural History of Lawyers

by Andrew & Jonathan Roth
National 1st Edition
This book is a painless and hilarious education, tracing the legal profession. Careful attention is given to the world's worst lawyers, most preposterous cases and most ludicrous courtroom strategies.
$12.95/DA

Poetic Justice: The Funniest, Meanest Things Ever Said About Lawyers

Edited by Jonathan & Andrew Roth
National 1st Edition
A great gift for anyone in the legal profession who has managed to maintain a sense of humor.
$8.95/PJ

RESEARCH & REFERENCE

Legal Research: How to Find and Understand the Law

Attorney Stephen Elias
National 2nd Edition
A valuable tool on its own or as a companion to just about every other Nolo book. This book gives easy-to-use, step-by-step instructions on how to find legal information.
$14.95/LRES

Family Law Dictionary

Attorneys Robin Leonard & Stephen Elias
National 2nd Edition
Finally, a legal dictionary that's written in plain English, not "legalese"! *The Family Law Dictionary* is designed to help the nonlawyer who has a question or problem involving family law—marriage, divorce, adoption or living together.
$13.95/FLD

A Dictionary of Patent, Copyright & Trademark Terms

Attorney Stephen Elias
National 2nd Edition
This book explains the terms associated with trade secrets, copyrights, trademarks, patents and contracts.
$15.95/IPLD

Legal Research Made Easy: A Roadmap Through the Law Library Maze

2-1/2 hr. videotape and 40-page manual
Nolo Press/Legal Star Communications
If you're a law student, paralegal or librarian—or just want to look up the law for yourself—this video is for you. University of California law professor Bob Berring explains how to use all the basic legal research tools in your local law library with an easy-to-follow six-step research plan and a sense of humor.
$89.95/LRME

SOFTWARE

WillMaker

Nolo Press/Legisoft
National 4th Edition
This easy-to-use software program lets you prepare and update a legal will—safely, privately and without the expense of a lawyer. Leading you step-by-step in a question-and-answer format, *WillMaker* builds a will around your answers, taking into account your state of residence. *WillMaker* comes with a 200-page legal manual which provides the legal background necessary to make sound choices. Good in all states except Louisiana.
IBM PC
(3-1/2 & 5-1/4 disks included) $69.95/WI4
MACINTOSH $69.95/WM4

For the Record

Carol Pladsen & Attorney Ralph Warner
National 2nd Edition
For the Record program provides a single place to keep a complete inventory of all your important legal, financial, personal and family records. It can compute your net worth and also create inventories of all insured property to protect your assets in the event of fire or theft. Includes a 200-page manual filled with practical and legal advice.
IBM PC
(3-1/2 & 5-1/4 disks included) $59.95/FRI2
MACINTOSH $59.95/FRM2

California Incorporator

Attorney Anthony Mancuso/Legisoft
California 1st Edition
Answer the questions on the screen and this software program will print out the 35-40 pages of documents you need to make your California corporation legal. Comes with a 200-page manual which explains the incorporation process.
IBM PC
(3-1/2 & 5-1/4 disks included) $129.00/INCI

The California Nonprofit Corporation Handbook

(computer edition)
Attorney Anthony Mancuso
California 1st Edition
This book/software package shows you step-by-step how to form and operate a nonprofit corporation in California. Included on disk are the forms for the Articles, Bylaws and Minutes.
IBM PC 5-1/4 $69.95/NPI
IBM PC 3-1/2 $69.95/NP3I
MACINTOSH $69.95/NPM

How to Form Your Own New York Corporation

How to Form Your Own Texas Corporation

Computer Editions
Attorney Anthony Mancuso
These book/software packages contain the instructions and tax information and forms you need to incorporate a small business and save hundreds of dollars in lawyers' fees. All organizational forms are on disk. Both come with a 250-page manual.

New York 1st Edition
IBM PC 5-1/4 $69.95/NYCI
IBM PC 3-1/2 $69.95/NYC3I
MACINTOSH $69.95/NYCM

Texas 1st Edition
IBM PC 5-1/4 $69.95/TCI
IBM PC 3-1/2 $69.95/TC3I
MACINTOSH $69.95/TCM

VISIT OUR STORE

If you live in the Bay Area, be sure to visit the Nolo Press Bookstore on the corner of 9th & Parker Streets in West Berkeley. You'll find our complete line of books and software—new and "damaged"—all at a discount. We also have t-shirts, posters and a selection of business and legal self-help books from other publishers.

HOURS

Monday to Friday	10 a.m. to 5 p.m.
Thursdays	Until 6 p.m
Saturdays	10 a.m. to 4:30 p.m.
Sundays	10 a.m. to 3 p.m.

950 Parker St., Berkeley, California 94710

ORDER FORM

Name

Address (UPS to street address, Priority Mail to P.O. boxes)

Catalog Code	Quantity	Item	Unit price	Total
		Subtotal		
		Sales tax (California residents only)		
		Shipping & handling		
		2nd day UPS		
		TOTAL		
		PRICES SUBJECT TO CHANGE		

SALES TAX
California residents add your local tax:
7 1/4, 7 3/4, 8 1/4

SHIPPING & HANDLING
$4.00 1 item
$5.00 2-3 items
+$.50 each additional item
Allow 2-3 weeks for delivery

IN A HURRY?
UPS 2nd day delivery is available:
Add $5.00 (contiguous states) or
$8.00 (Alaska & Hawaii) to your regular shipping and handling charges

FOR FASTER SERVICE, USE YOUR CREDIT CARD AND OUR TOLL-FREE NUMBERS:
Monday-Friday, 7 a.m. to 5 p.m. Pacific Time

US	1 (800) 992-6656
CA (outside 510 area code)	1 (800) 640-6656
(inside 510 area code)	549-1976
General Information	1 (510) 549-1976
Fax us your order	1 (510) 548-5902

METHOD OF PAYMENT
☐ Check enclosed
☐ VISA ☐ Mastercard ☐ Discover Card ☐ American Expre

Account # Expiration Date

Signature Authorizing

Phone

CONT

For the Record 2.0

Software available for IBM (3 1/2" and 5 1/4" disks included) and Macintosh

By Carol Pladsen & Ralph Warner

$59.95

Gets you organized at last

If your family records are scattered among a half dozen file folders, a stack of manila envelopes (some bulging at the seams), and a shoe box or two of miscellaneous papers stacked precariously on the second shelf of the hall closet, you need this program. With *For the Record,* your personal, financial and legal matters records are stored in one place, making it easy to retrieve them whenever you need to.

Prompts you to record anything you might have forgotten

For the Record's customized screens create a place for all the important information in your life: credit card numbers, emergency and medical information, insurance records, deeds, business interests, tax records, facts about collectibles, personal and family history, and much more.

Special features include home inventory reports for insurance purposes and net worth calculations, and on-screen notepads which let you record any miscellaneous information that may be relevant to a particular entry. Cross-references help you find related information.

Allows you to share your records or keep them private

You can print out your *For the Record* files and give them to a trusted relative or friend, or you can keep information private in a locked file in your computer with your own designated password.

Manual includes valuable legal and consumer information

The 200-page *For the Record* manual offers hundreds of legal and practical tips on record-keeping and financial planning on everything from where to store your will to how to shop for a credit card.

"Every family ought to get a copy."

—San Jose Mercury News

"It's superb for the job it was designed to do."

—MacUser

"This is a dandy little package for collecting all your records and data in one place."

—BYTE

TO ORDER USE THE ORDER FORM ON THE PRECEDING PAGE OR CALL US TOLL FREE:

1-800-992-6656	**U.S. (OUTSIDE CA)**
1-800-640-6656	**CA (OUTSIDE 510 AREA)**
549-1976	**(INSIDE 510 AREA)**

Update Service

RECYCLE YOUR OUT-OF-DATE BOOKS AND GET 25% OFF YOUR NEXT PURCHASE!

It's important to have the most current legal information. Because laws and legal procedures change often, we update our books regularly. To help keep you up-to-date we are extending this special offer: Send or bring us the title portion of the cover of any old Nolo book and we'll give you a 25% discount off the retail price of any new Nolo book! You'll find current prices and an order form at the back of this book. Generally speaking, any book more than two years old is of questionable value. Books more than four or five years old are usually a menace. This offer is to individuals only.

OUT-OF-DATE = DANGEROUS

CONT 9/91

FREE NOLO NEWS SUBSCRIPTION

When you register, we'll send you our quarterly newspaper, the *Nolo News,* free for two years. (U.S. addresses only.) Here's what you'll get in every issue:

INFORMATIVE ARTICLES

Written by Nolo editors, articles provide practical legal information on issues you encounter in everyday life: family law, wills, debts, consumer rights, and much more.

UPDATE SERVICE

The *Nolo News* keeps you informed of legal changes that affect any Nolo book and software program.

BOOK AND SOFTWARE REVIEWS

We're always looking for good legal and consumer books and software from other publishers. When we find them, we review them and offer them in our mail order catalog.

ANSWERS TO YOUR LEGAL QUESTIONS

Our readers are always challenging us with good questions on a variety of legal issues. So in each issue, "Auntie Nolo" gives sage advice and sound information.

COMPLETE NOLO PRESS CATALOG

The *Nolo News* contains an up-to-the-minute catalog of all Nolo books and software, which you can order using our toll-free "800" order line. And you can see at a glance if you're using an out-of-date version of a Nolo product.

LAWYER JOKES

Nolo's famous lawyer joke column continually gets the goat of the legal establishment. If we print a joke you send in, you'll get a $20 Nolo gift certificate.

We promise *never* to give your name and address to any other organization.

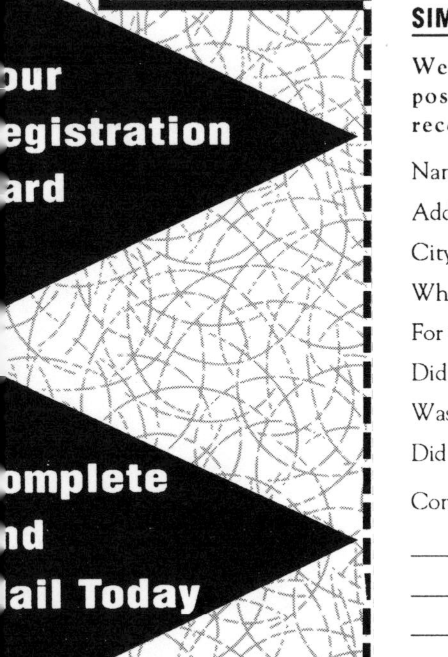

SIMPLE CONTRACTS FOR PERSONAL USE — Registration Card

We'd like to know what you think! Please take a moment to fill out and return this postage paid card for a free two-year subscription to the *Nolo News*. If you already receive the *Nolo News*, we'll extend your subscription.

Name ____________________ Ph.( ) __________

Address ____________________

City ____________________ State ______ Zip __________

Where did you hear about this book? ____________________

For what purpose did you use this book? ____________________

Did you consult a lawyer?	Yes	No	Not Applicable				
Was it easy for you to use this book?	(very easy)	5	4	3	2	1	(very difficult)
Did you find this book helpful?	(very)	5	4	3	2	1	(not at all)

Comments ____________________

THANK YOU — CONT 2

[Nolo books are]..."written in plain language, free of legal mumbo jumbo, and spiced with witty personal observations."

—ASSOCIATED PRESS

"Well-produced and slickly written, the [Nolo] books are designed to take the mystery out of seemingly involved procedures, carefully avoiding legalese and leading the reader step-by-step through such everyday legal problems as filling out forms, making up contracts, and even how to behave in court."

—SAN FRANCISCO EXAMINER

"...Nolo publications...guide people simply through the how, when, where and why of law."

—WASHINGTON POST

"Increasingly, people who are not lawyers are performing tasks usually regarded as legal work... And consumers, using books like Nolo's, do routine legal work themselves."

—NEW YORK TIMES

"...All of [Nolo's] books are easy-to-understand, are updated regularly, provide pull-out forms...and are often quite moving in their sense of compassion for the struggles of the lay reader."

—SAN FRANCISCO CHRONICLE